D1542651

Beer for
ALL SEASONS

# Beer for
## ALL SEASONS

### RANDY MOSHER

Storey Publishing

*The mission of Storey Publishing is to serve our customers by publishing practical information that encourages personal independence in harmony with the environment.*

EDITED BY Margaret Sutherland
ART DIRECTION AND BOOK DESIGN BY Carolyn Eckert
COVER DESIGN BY de Vicq Design
TEXT PRODUCTION BY Liseann Karandisecky
INDEXED BY Nancy D. Wood

ILLUSTRATIONS BY © Owen Davey/Folio Illustration Agency, except page 33 by Randy Mosher and Dan O. Williams and pages 72, 73, and 152 by © Randy Mosher
COASTER DESIGNS ON MONTHLY ROUNDUP PAGES AND SPINE GRAPHIC BY de Vicq Design
COVER AND INTERIOR PHOTOGRAPHY BY Mars Vilaubi, © Storey Publishing, except as credited on page 199.

Thank you to The Dirty Truth, Northampton, MA, for providing a great bar for our location photography.

Storey Publishing
210 MASS MoCA Way
North Adams, MA 01247
www.storey.com

Printed in China by R.R. Donnelley
10 9 8 7 6 5 4 3 2 1

Library of Congress Cataloging-in-Publication Data
Mosher, Randy.
 Beer for all seasons : a through-the-year
    guide to what to drink and when to
    drink it / by Randy Mosher.
   pages cm
 Includes index.
 ISBN 978-1-61212-347-9 (pbk. : alk. paper)
 ISBN 978-1-61212-348-6 (ebook) 1. Beer–
History. I. Title.
TP577.M675 2015
641.2'3–dc23
                                    2014033701

## DEDICATION
### FOR NANCY

## ACKNOWLEDGMENTS
Thanks to the fabulous team at
Storey that put in a lot of extra
work to make this book a visual
gem, and who make it a genuine
pleasure to be a writer. Thanks
also to Greg Koch for his foreword.

CONT

ENTS

# BEER FOR SEASONS, SEASONS FOR BEERS

**T**HIS, **AT ITS CORE,** is a subject I simultaneously embrace and find myself at odds with.

You see, a part of me loves the idea of seasonality in beer. I get to look forward to different flavor profiles coming and going with the leaves on the trees. And yet another part of me simply wants to drink any beer at any time I damn well please.

Before the craft-brewing revolution (and still today), where were some of the most famous strong stouts brewed? Why, they were all brewed in colder-climate countries, of course. Who wants to drink a 7% stout in a hot and humid climate? No one!

Oh really? That's not the case at all, my friends. In fact, I fibbed to you just a few sentences ago. I intentionally set you up to nod in agreement at a false statement. The truth is that before the craft-brewing revolution some of the most famous stronger stouts (strong by pre-craft-brewing standards, that is) were brewed and sold in hot and humid countries. Lion Stout comes from Sri Lanka. Face-meltingly hot and humid Southeast Asia has three major brands of 7%+ stouts. Dragon Stout, from Jamaica, comes in at 7.5% ABV.

I've often heard newly minted beer enthusiasts state with great authority that there are few greater beer faux pas than drinking a stout when the thermometer goes above 60°F. They proclaim this without realizing that in much of the world a strong stout is not considered a seasonal beer. Hell, in those countries I mentioned they drink a (comparatively) large amount of strong stout and yet they barely even have seasons!

In some respects, the seasonality effect is quite similar to the origin effect. In short, nothing more than marketing hype that trades in the currency of imagined attributes over actual attributes and differentiation. Now before you write this off as just another curmudgeonly Gregism, intent on ruining the warm and fuzzies that some folks get when they buy into these marketing schemes, stick with me here for a moment, and I'll explain.

Origin effect, or the imagination of it, is no better represented than in this question I sometimes like to ask at Japanese restaurants: What exactly is it about a beer brand that was started by Americans with a German brewer in Japan, later sold to the Japanese, and now brewed in Los Angeles, California, that makes said beer go better with sushi? Answer: the fact that people perceive it as a Japanese beer. There's no actual demonstrative thing that makes that beer go better with that food.

Perhaps that's why my favorite sushi restaurant in San Diego County focuses simply on hiring sushi chefs with talent and dedication, rather than by their ethnicity. That, and they also only serve sustainable fish. And they also focus on craft beer. And organic local produce. In other words, they focus on doing an excellent job, rather than just playing into preconceived notions by some customers as to what a sushi restaurant should be. No wonder it's a fantastic place.

And that, my friends, is the rub. Focus on excellence, as Randy does in his through-the-year survey of craft beers, and all else falls into place. Focus on image, and you'll be wading in shallower waters. And what's the fun in that? Shallow waters are for toddlers.

The best of all worlds? Well, that's in this delightful tome covering the occurrences when season, authenticity, and good taste all find themselves saddled up to the bar or dinner table at the same time.

Cheers,
**GREG KOCH**
*CEO and cofounder*
*Stone Brewing Co.*
*Stone Brewing World Bistro & Gardens*

# CHAPTER ONE

## BEER. ×HISTORY×

## & AGRICULTURE

# All human life once revolved around the seasons. There was no other way. Nature dominated; our forebears had to adapt or be left behind. Each year was a grand cycle of migrations, fertility, hardship, and renewal. There was prey to be stalked, fruit to be gathered, and gods to appease. Being in tune with the seasons was a matter of life and death for these early people.

As our ancestors came down from the hills and settled into an agricultural existence on the fertile riverbanks, they gained some measure of control, but the new way of life did not diminish the importance of the seasons. Crops had to be timed to the rain and the sun, and the animals they sheltered had their own seasonal patterns. People looked to the heavens for guidance, reciprocating with rituals and offerings to ensure the smooth workings of the cosmos. To this day, religion remains highly connected to the cyclical flow of time and the events it hopes to conjure to fruition. It's embedded in our spiritual DNA.

During the birth of agricultural life about 10,000 years ago, beer appeared. It is not precisely known what role it played in our own domestication, but having a ready supply of alcohol must have been an irresistible incentive to settle down and abandon the nomadic life. Beyond its obvious charms, beer appears to have been used as an incentive to draw people together for periodic feasts and festivals, building prestige for their hosts and helping to connect widespread communities into tribes and nations through trade, the exchange of ideas, matchmaking, and general merrymaking. It would appear that the beer bash is nearly as old as beer itself. In some ways, beer retains its social power, as is evident during any beer festival today.

As an agricultural product, beer ebbed and flowed with the seasons in well-defined ways. At harvest time, new malt and other ingredients such as hops became available for brewing. Each component of beer has a specific rhythm: cultivation, ripening, harvesting, processing into storage, and its ultimate use in the brew pot. Some ingredients — especially hops — are perishable and start to fade as soon as they are picked, making the first beers of the brewing season something special.

## FAST-MATURING small beers were enjoyed as summer refreshment.

While the new plants were growing, it was hot, and as a result, summer was never a desirable time for brewing. There was no one available to brew anyway, because most of the available workers were needed in the fields. Summer's warmth makes it difficult to conduct clean fermentations, and this problem is exacerbated by large amounts of wild microbes wafting through the air. Except for the British Isles, where temperatures were a bit cooler, summer brewing in Europe was often restricted — sometimes by force of law — to weak, fast-maturing small beers intended solely to be enjoyed as summer refreshment and a source of safe, potable water.

For most of Europe, full-strength beers were brewed only in the period between October and March or April, when cooler temperatures encouraged a slow, clean fermentation with a long maturation period for the stronger beers. Such beers were sometimes named for the month of their brewing. In England,

Hacker Märzen
ORIGINAL MÜNCHNER OKTOBERFESTBIER

*real* beer, so October beer was quite special. Similar "March beers" were brewed, but these were thought somewhat inferior, as the hops had lost a little of their freshness in the interim.

Germany still brews Märzen beers, most typically associated with Oktoberfest; bières de Mars may be found in France and Belgium. Both are named for the month of March and have their origins in spring-brewed beers that were aged, or lagered, in cool cellars through the summer. Märzen was tapped for harvest festivals and became the beery core of Munich's Oktoberfest nearly from its beginning in 1810.

These harvest-related specialties were just part of the cycle of beer. Through the depths of winter and well into spring, strong beers came to the table after a long conditioning period. The English term *winter warmer* sums up these beers perfectly, and in the chilly days before central heating, the term was no mere metaphor.

Much of life in preindustrial Europe revolved around the religious calendar, and some traditional styles reflect this. In Germany, the promise of spring and perhaps the bending of some religious rules surrounding Lenten fasting produced

"October beer" was the hoppy, amber strong ale most famously brewed on country estates and aged for a year or more before being served. Brewed with little regard for expense from the freshest hops and malt on private estates, it was universally considered the best beer in Britain. After months of small beer, brewers would have been thrilled to get back to the business of brewing the flesh-sustaining strong lager doppelbock. As spring arrives, we see celebratory Easter beers in northern Europe, followed by the balanced beauty of German mai-bock. And with or without religion, on that first warm day the picnic tables come out and with them the luminously hazy hefeweizen, Berliner Weisse, or Belgian witbier, as well as other summer beers that will sustain and refresh us until the cycle begins again.

With all these traditions, it's clear that seasonality in beer was not a whim but a functional necessity, deeply embedded into the social

fabric of the day. Technology has empowered us to ignore the reality outside our windows, but it is not that much fun to live our lives totally cocooned. No matter how much "progress" we have made, we still enjoy the cycle of the seasons, as they bring variety and create special moments and seasonal products to look forward to, especially an ever-changing selection of beers to drink.

**Mardi Gras has been a drinking occasion for ages.**

# THE PURPOSES OF BEER

**R**EFRESHING, sustaining, convivial, and delicious, beer has served many roles almost from the very beginning, sustaining us in many ways — "meat and drink and cloth" as the English put it. Even the ancient Sumerians had small (low-alcohol) everyday beer and medium-strength table beer as well as luxury beers and even a special lower-calorie beer called *eb-la*, literally meaning "lessens the waist."

And so it has been for most of beer's history, right up until modern times, when scale and efficiency dictated that a single type of beer — yellow, fizzy, and easy to drink — would suit everybody's needs, not just for mowing the lawn but for every other occasion as well. Fortunately, things have changed. There are abundant choices available almost everywhere, and more are coming as the revolution spreads. Craft beer is booming even in places that were quite recently utter beer deserts, so in today's world you have no excuse for not drinking with the seasons. But at any given moment, what do you really *want*?

Outdoor activities in the heat of summer call for light, tangy, and refreshing beers. Despite the surge of strong, bitter beers from many craft brewers, there is a counter trend that focuses on more session-friendly beers to enjoy by the gulp rather than the sip. It takes a little more cleverness to create a delicate, refreshing beer that still delivers a lot of flavor, but it can be done, as anyone who has ever had a beer in England, Germany, Belgium, or the Czech Republic knows. Brewers have tricks for making a modest beer seem more flavorful. Great-quality malts and some fine hop aromas are one way, and that gets you into pilsner, bitter, or Kölsch territory. The rich and creamy, yet dry, character of wheat has long been the basis of many summertime beers, from Bavarian hefeweizen to Belgian witbier and a host of less famous beers that were once beloved throughout the northern regions of continental Europe. A touch of acidity doesn't hurt, either, as Berliner Weisse demonstrates.

No matter the weather, there is always a need for beers that suit the dining table. These are of middling strength, around 5 or 6 percent alcohol by volume (ABV), and every brewing culture since the dawn of beer has something in this range. Weaker or stronger beers can find food partners, for sure, but in this middle range, beer very graciously interacts with most meals. Given the huge range of flavors and aromas available, there are plenty of opportunities to find connections between beer and whatever is on the plate.

Weighty and carb-rich beers were once commonplace. Often regarded as "liquid bread," they really did serve that purpose when meat was a luxury and the hard physical work of the day demanded a high caloric intake. Today, strong, rich beers are specialty items; perhaps the term *liquid dessert* is more appropriate. With our rich daily diet, such beers are counterproductive, so over the past 150 years the general trend has been toward beers that are lighter on the palate and much less weighty.

# DRINKING WITH THE RHYTHM OF THE SEASONS

**T**HE YOU WHO BROWSES the refrigerated shelves in the heat of summer may be a very different you than the person who stops to pick up something toothsome for the holidays. Every season has its beers, and drinking seasonally helps us stay in touch with the ebb and flow of life and connects us to those who came before us who had similar desires for something refreshing, warming, profound, bracing, or whatever is our

heart's desire. There are hundreds, if not thousands, of great choices waiting to satisfy every beery urge.

Whether you're actually mowing the lawn or not, the heat of the summer demands beers that are refreshing and not too alcoholic. Most are pale in color, but there are quenching dark beers such as Irish stout and Düsseldorfer altbier, to name two. In the midst of the season's agricultural bounty, a fruit beer might hit the spot. As the heat of day fades into a glorious summer night, the bracing herbal hoppiness of an IPA could be a great choice, or possibly a hoppy American stout.

As the days shorten and the first chilly breeze of fall blasts through, more substantial beers come to the fore. A rich and malty Märzen the color of turning leaves is iconic for the season. A smoked version of the same might conjure up memories of campfires or burning leaves. Pumpkin ale, with its warm spiciness, is a harbinger of the pies and gingerbread to come as the season deepens.

As the weather becomes cooler and darker by degrees, tastes shift to bigger, darker, more sustaining beers. The holidays demand a certain celebratory spin, and then it's on to the business of surviving the winter, made possible by a small glass of something strong and dark by the fireplace as the winds howl outside.

Valentine's Day signifies the promise of new life and gives us a reason for another celebratory moment in a season that really needs as many as it can get. It's a special opportunity for an elegant and luxurious beer. As the winter ebbs in fits and starts, never warming quickly enough for us, the beers become brighter, paler, more full of hope, until finally there's that first truly warm day and it's time to break out something nearly summery, drinking in the fleeting preview of what's to come.

This cycle of beers ties us to something bigger than our short-lived whims and provides some structure for our explorations. As each new round of seasonal beers pops up in the stores, the beer landscape changes, mirroring the world outside.

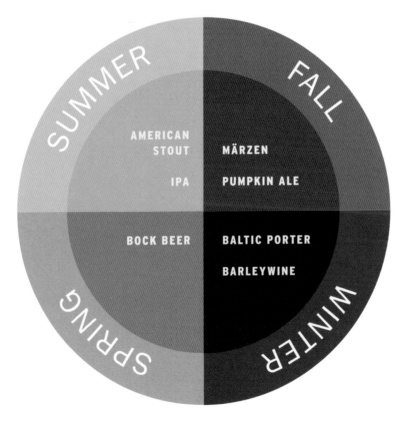

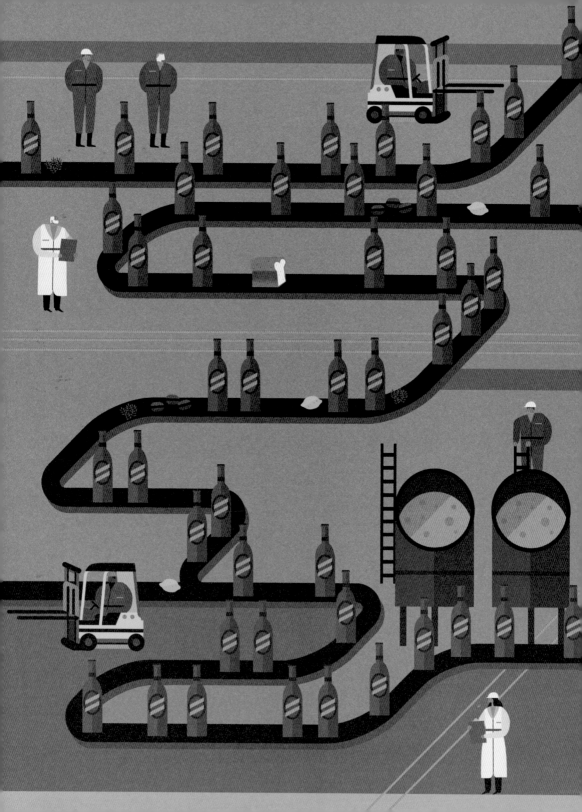

CH. TWO

GETTING THE MOST
from
YOUR YEAR
of BEER

# 𝕭eer can be enjoyed without any understanding of its inner workings or methods of production. Sometimes it's great to mindlessly kick back and just *enjoy* a beer without analyzing it to death. On the other hand, a well-brewed beer is a deliciously layered and complex product, displaying a vast range of styles, strengths, colors, intensities, textures, and other qualities. It helps to have a little insight into its history, components, manufacture, and sensory qualities to fully appreciate its depths.

Every beer tells a story about its agricultural roots, chemistry, brewing process, measured parameters, sensory qualities, historical context, and more. It's helpful to have a grasp of how all these qualities relate to the liquid in the glass. Untangling beer's complexity can be daunting, but if you break it down into manageable pieces, the whole picture will start to come together. Just remember to keep a glass of something foamy and delicious handy as you learn, to remind you of the rewards for all this hard work.

## A WORKING VOCABULARY OF BEER FLAVOR

**F**LAVOR SHOULD BE the starting point of any enthusiast's beer knowledge. No matter what the context, it always comes down to just you and that beer coming to terms with each other. You can read a lot of history, study the style guidelines, absorb other people's reviews and opinions, and more, but without a firm grasp of the flavors that beer presents to the senses, it won't mean much. Your journey starts here.

Take a whiff of that ale. Fruity, you say? That's a good start, but can you break it down a little more? In the tasting world, we strive to be as specific as possible. What kind of fruit? Berries? White fruit, like pears? Dried or fresh fruit? Maybe something tropical? That's good, but can you go deeper? Pineapple, passion fruit, bananas? If it's the last, you might go one more step and name the molecule, in this case an ester called isoamyl acetate, which is common in fermentation and is a defining characteristic of Bavarian wheat beers or hefeweizens.

Every one of the aromas and flavors we can detect in beer has its origins in the biochemical processes within the raw ingredients plus the processes that create and modify them during brewing and fermentation. With 1,300 flavor chemicals known to exist in beer, it is impossible to be on first-name terms with more than a small percentage. But

with some practice, anyone can develop a familiarity with beer's many tastes, textures, and aromas. Becoming a serious taster can take a lifetime of study, and while there is no final destination, you can make measurable progress on your journey. I can tell you that it takes a lot of work to get to where you really want to be but that the long and winding road is a joy to ride.

## MALT: THE HEART OF BEER

Malt is a product that is created by the controlled sprouting of barley or other grains. As the seed sprouts, it unleashes a host of changes in structure, composition, and flavor. As the nascent plant readies its energy reserves for the formidable task of building itself anew, it activates enzymes, breaks down storage structures, and prepares to transform from a dormant seed into a vital, growing plant. These

changes allow us to bend the barley to our will, hijacking its enzymes and gaining access to its starches. During the brewing process, these starches break down into simple sugars to make wort with which to feed the yeast. The yeast will turn the mix into beer, creating alcohol and much more in the process.

The malting process lasts for about a week. While the changes it creates are central to the brewing process, the early stages of malting don't create a lot of flavor. It is only during the final step, the kilning, that the malt flavor really comes into bloom. Just as a loaf of unbaked bread is pretty lifeless and unappetizing until it is baked to a beautifully aromatic brown, malt needs the heat of a kiln to create the rich, warm, complex flavors we love in beer.

Kilning creates a dual bounty of complex aroma chemicals and those that lend a wide range of color to malt. When heat is applied to sugar or starch mixed with nitrogenous material such as the proteins found in malt, a type of browning called the Maillard reaction occurs. It is the most important chemical process in the browning of any food, from sautéed onions or grilled meat to baked cookies or milk caramel. Most flavors and browned colors in cooked food come from the complex chemical reactions of the Maillard process.

There is another type of browning that does not involve nitrogen, known simply as caramelization. Flavors involved here tend toward burnt sugar or toasted marshmallow. They are most common in caramel malts that are kilned after

> **There are dozens of different malt types available to brewers, and each has its own unique set of flavors.**

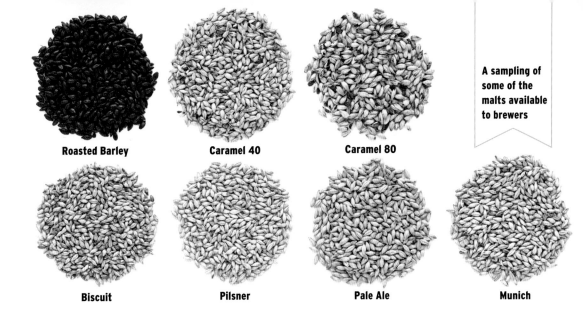

**Roasted Barley**  **Caramel 40**  **Caramel 80**

**Biscuit**  **Pilsner**  **Pale Ale**  **Munich**

they develop a lot of simple sugars, and they provide unique raisiny and burnt sugar flavors. Browning also occurs in the brewing process, especially in the boiling kettle; special brewing processes such as decoction enhance this activity.

The chemistry of kilning is terrifyingly complex. Even with the same starting materials, every set of conditions, including time, temperature, pH, and moisture level, creates a different mix of flavors. By manipulating the kilning process as well as the material that goes into it, a maltster can transform a single type of barley into dozens of distinctly different malts that a brewer can use as a start for formulating a recipe.

The malt flavor vocabulary terms we use to describe beer reflect the universality of Maillard browning in cooking: *bread, cracker, biscuit, caramel, toffee, raisins, nuts, toast, roast, coffee, chocolate, espresso.* With these terms we have a pretty good match between the words we use and what we can actually experience from malt in the finished beer. If you're new to this flavor vocabulary and want to know more, I highly recommend going to a homebrew shop and purchasing several different types of malt, such as pilsner, pale ale, Munich, biscuit, caramel (in two different colors, maybe 40 and 80), and perhaps a roasted malt. You can simply pop them into your mouth and taste them, or crush them lightly and make a tea with a little hot water.

A Pocket of Hops.

## HOPS: THE SOUL OF BEER

Hops are the papery, cone-like fruits of a climbing vine. They have been continuously used in beer for more than a thousand years, replacing the bitter herbs that preceded them and helped along by the fact that hops have some preservative value that the older bittering herbs, such as bog myrtle, lack. Unlike those of barley malt, hop aromas are created mostly by the plant itself. Once harvested, the changes in hops are mostly negative — simple deterioration during processing and storage. Bitterness develops as a result of a chemical change called isomerization, which occurs when the hops are boiled during brewing. Hops provide a pleasing bitterness as a counterpoint to malt's richness, along with aromas ranging from floral to citrus to herbal.

Many biochemical processes can occur across differing plant species, so the flavors in hops that strike us as piney or citrus or herbal are provided by some of the same aromatic chemicals that are found in evergreens, citrus fruit, and herbs. There are more than 200 different aromatic chemicals known in hops, and we don't have the words needed to describe them all. And of course they're interacting with each other in a beer, making it even more difficult to untangle the many similar aromas. The best thing we can do is try to note what impression jumps out when we get our first whiff of them in the beer.

Positive attributes include citrus (lemon, lime, grapefruit, orange), grassy, piney, floral (lavender, geranium, marigold), herbal (mint, oregano, rosemary, thyme), and spicy, a term we use to describe the Saaz and related hop varieties, although their aromas really have very little to do with spice. Hops may present some negative flavors as well, like catty (like cat pee) and onion/garlic (like onion powder, not fresh), and if hops are exposed to heat and oxygen during storage, a stinky cheese aroma can develop.

Just as with malt, it may be helpful to purchase some different hops and smell them or make up some simple teas to sniff. The availability of hop varieties changes, so just tell your homebrew shop what you want to do with them, and they'll help you make a selection..

The bitterness hops provide is of supreme importance in beer, and this aspect of their flavor could not be simpler to describe: bitter. While aromas and flavors may be vastly different between hop varieties, the bitterness they provide is all exactly the same.

## FERMENTATION AND FLAVOR

The single-celled fungus we call brewer's yeast metabolizes sugar, producing ethyl alcohol and carbon dioxide. If it really were this simple, beer would be a lifeless and fairly bland product. Fortunately, as it ferments our beer for us, yeast churns out hundreds of flavor chemicals. Yeast is quite a complex little creature, employing a huge array of biochemical processes in its business of staying alive and reproducing, but it's a bit sloppy about cleaning up after itself. Depending on temperature, genetics, and a number of other conditions, yeast releases many volatile chemicals into the beer, affecting the overall flavor and aroma of the finished product. Beyond the characteristics of the yeast strain itself, the most important of these variables is temperature. The warmer the fermentation, the more of these ancillary flavor chemicals that are released, and that means a more complex aroma.

**Malted barley and yeast**

Bavarian hefeweizen comes from a *S. cerevisiae* strain sometimes called *Torulaspora delbrueckii*. Various wild yeasts, especially in the *Brettanomyces* genus, may be present in a few types of Belgian-style specialty beers, which may employ some bacteria as well.

The broad division between ales and lagers is mainly about temperature. Lager yeast is different mainly in its tolerance of low temperatures, which keep the flavors simple and pure. Because lager strains tend to do their work near the bottom of the tanks, they are called bottom-fermenting. Ale yeasts are top-fermenting, because of their preferred habitat.

Yeast flavor is strongly driven by genetics. There are hundreds of strains within the main species, *Saccharomyces cerevisiae*, and there are a few additional species that also are used in beer. Lager yeast is *S. pastorianus*; the familiar banana plus bubble gum plus clove of

**Ale or lager – can you tell by looking? Both come in all colors.**

# BEER BY THE NUMBERS

**W**HILE THE TOTAL experience that is a sip of beer cannot be completely broken down into numbers, there are a few important parameters that brewers regularly measure for quality control, stylistic, or other purposes. These numbers are also used in product literature, competition guidelines, and other contexts. Every beer enthusiast should understand what they mean.

First is original gravity, sometimes also referred to as extract. Before being fermented by yeast and becoming beer, the sugar-rich liquid created by the brewing process is called wort. Its density, or solids content, helps determine the final alcohol content after fermentation. This density is easily measured by a simple instrument called a hydrometer, or by more sophisticated laboratory tools in large-scale breweries.

There are two main systems for expressing original gravity. One uses sugar content as a percentage of total weight. This is a scale called degrees Plato, which is more or less the same as the Brix scale used in winemaking. So, for example, 10 percent solids equals 10 degrees Plato — often shortened to simply °P. Most large breweries use this scale, which originated in the lager-brewing heartland of Europe. You may still see references to the Balling scale, an earlier and slightly less accurate scale, which was replaced some time ago by the Plato scale.

The other gravity scale is British, and it expresses the density of the liquid relative to the weight of pure water. This produces a different-looking number with four digits, a decimal point, and the letters *OG* (meaning original gravity) before or after: for example, 1.040 OG. It means that a 1.040 wort will be 1.04 times as dense as pure water, weighing 1.04 grams per cubic centimeter. Still common in British breweries, this is the scale most often used by American homebrewers, since British homebrew literature was omnipresent when the hobby was really getting rolling in the 1980s.

The two scales can be converted back and forth. A reliable rule that works at the lower end of the scale is that the last two OG numbers (for example, in 1.040 gravity, use the

40) divided by 4 roughly equals °P (in this case, 10 °P).

Ethanol, or ethyl alcohol, in beer is generally measured worldwide in percent by volume, sometimes listed as % ABV or % alc/vol. This is the current U.S. federal standard, and it is used in most other countries as well. Confusingly, percentage by weight is sometimes used, especially according to U.S. state laws. Its use is the result of a post-Prohibition decision by brewers to find a scale to express alcohol content in the smallest-looking number. So, alcohol in a 4% ABV beer is only 3.2% by weight. When U.S. and Canadian brewers were using different units of measure, this discrepancy gave rise to the myth that Canadian beer was stronger.

Gravity and alcohol content are related, but only indirectly, as not all of the solids dissolved in wort will ferment. The brewer has a fair degree of control over this, manipulating the brewing process to affect the sweetness or dryness of the finished beer. *Attenuation* is the term used to express how much of the wort solids actually ferment. The precise method is to distill and carefully weigh the alcohol and then perform a calculation yielding a number called real attenuation. However, it is far simpler to divide the ending gravity by the starting gravity, resulting in a percentage figure known as apparent attenuation. Because it's so much easier to calculate, apparent attenuation is used by smaller breweries. The reason the two are not the same is that the alcohol in the finished beer, being less dense than water, distorts the reading, so it is possible to have an apparent attenuation of over 100 percent.

From a tasting perspective, attenuation affects the sweetness or dryness of the beer. Poorly attenuated styles such as Scottish ales or doppelbocks have a lot of residual

The hydrometer measures the original gravity of beer. The scale is read at the level of the liquid surface.

**High attenuation = crisp, dry beer**

**Low attenuation = rich, sweet beer**

unfermented sugar. Pilsners, saisons, and strong Belgian ales are usually fairly well attenuated, with a drier palate. Light, dry, and ice beers are super-attenuated beers for which their brewers have to use industrial enzymes derived from fungi to break down all the malt carbohydrates into fermentable sugars.

# TASTING EXPERTISE

**ECOMING A BETTER** taster is a never-ending journey through both the senses and learning about the many complex processes that go into the manu-

facture of beer. Reading is a good start, but critical tasting requires an entirely different kind of learning. Books can give you a good framework on which to hang your experiences, but it's the physical act of getting your nose into the glass and the beer onto your palate that turns a drinker into a taster.

While it is possible to proceed on your own, it's very helpful — and a whole lot more fun — to do this in the company of like-minded travelers. Judging beer is the ultimate training for a serious taster. Putting a study group together to prepare for a certification exam such as the Cicerone — the beer world's equivalent to the sommelier exam — or the BJCP (Beer Judge Certification Program) — for homebrewing

## Tasting Record

| | |
|---|---|
| **DATE** | **TASTED BY** |
| **BEER** | **AGE OF BEER** |
| **TYPE/STYLE** | **PACKAGE** |
| **LOCATION** | **ALCOHOL/GRAVITY** |
| **AROMA** | **Specific off-flavors and aroma** |
| **APPEARANCE** | ○ Acetaldehyde<br>○ Acetic<br>○ Acidic (Vinegar)<br>○ Alcoholic<br>○ Astringent/Harsh |
| **BODY & TEXTURE** | ○ Barnyard<br>○ Earthy/Corked<br>○ Cheesy<br>○ Chlorophenol (bandage)<br>○ Diacetyl (buttery)<br>○ DMS (creamed corn) |
| **AFTERTASTE** | ○ Estery/Solvently<br>○ Goaty/Sweaty<br>○ Metallic<br>○ Phenolic<br>○ Oxidized |
| **OVERALL IMPRESSIONS** | ○ Skunked<br>○ Sulfuric/Sulfidic<br>○ Yeasty/Autolysed<br>○ Other |

**A sample score sheet for judging beer**

contest judges — is immensely helpful and highly convivial. We all perceive things differently, so having a small group tasting the same beer and offering different points of view yields many useful insights. To stay sharp, tasting requires frequent practice, and the structured format of competition judging focuses the mind in ways that no casual sipping ever will. I never walk away from a judging table without feeling that I've learned something utterly new and unexpected.

## YOUR BRAIN ON BEER

It is obvious that we confront beer with our senses, but it's important to acquire a working knowledge of how our senses operate as they interact with beer. Each sense responds to stimuli via particular biochemical mechanisms, sending that information to the brain through pathways and processes that are only now beginning to be understood. The brain is stupendously complex. It thinks, feels, acts, recalls, judges, calculates, predicts, responds, and synthesizes, all simultaneously. All these processes and more are active when we taste beer.

It helps to break down the beer-tasting experience into individual senses, while recognizing that there is plenty of interaction among the senses. The light reflected by beer strikes our eyes while it interacts with our chemical senses, but these impulses are just the very first steps on a long path of perception traveling through different parts of our brain before becoming conscious thoughts. How we process, organize, and interpret those sensations is conditioned not only by hundreds of millions of years of evolution, but also by our own life histories, right up to the moment we take a sip.

We'll break that all down into a little more detail to get you started on your tasting journey.

*Taste* refers to the processes that occur mainly on the tongue but that are also active elsewhere in your mouth to a lesser extent. Everyone knows that sweet, salty, sour, and bitter are primary tastes detected by sensory cells called taste buds. However, science has uncovered more: umami, a savory taste that is a marker for protein; fat; carbonation; metallic ions like iron and copper; and kokumi, a still disputed quality similar to umami. It is likely that there will be more discoveries before we have a complete list.

Contrary to popular conception, the different tastes are fairly evenly distributed on the front half of the tongue, not in concentrated areas for each taste like the old tongue taste map showed. There are areas on the sides of the tongue toward the back that are more sensitive to sourness, and another area at the very back edge of the tongue that is a bit more sensitive to bitterness, umami, and perhaps sweetness as well.

Like all our senses, taste has evolved to help us understand our environment and keep us properly fed and safe. It is so critical to our survival that there are three pathways to the brain, so that if one should become damaged, we still have backups. Once leaving the tongue, one of the first places the taste signals reach is the brain stem, the most primitive

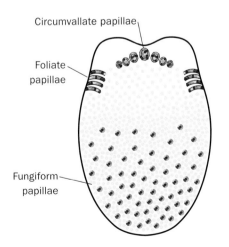

Circumvallate papillae

Foliate papillae

Fungiform papillae

- ● **UMAMI**
- ● **SOUR**
- ○ **SALTY**
- ● **SWEET**
- ● **BITTER**

Fat and other sensitivities not shown for clarity's sake.

Filiform papillae (no taste buds)

A modern tongue map no longer assigns specific tastes to particular areas of the tongue.

part of our brain, which controls heartbeat and respiration, among other things. It is the brain stem that makes the judgment as to whether a taste is pleasant or not.

Each different taste has a specific mechanism for triggering a nerve impulse, and these may range from lightning-quick in the case of salt and sour to somewhat slower for tastes such as bitterness and umami. This is important, because it forces us to think of the tasting act as having a time dimension. We'll come back to that.

In addition to taste, your mouth has a system of sensory nerves that can detect textures and chemical stimuli. Because beer has a lot of textural qualities, this is an important quality, giving us information about mouthfeel, carbonation, body, heat, cold, chile heat, menthol, and astringency. These nerves are fed by a branching structure called the trigeminal nerve, so these mouth sensations are usually called trigeminal sensations.

The perception of aroma is a good deal more complex, both in the number of smells — or as scientists say, odorants — that can be perceived as well as in the way the sense connects to the brain. Humans have the ability to detect about 10,000 different aromas. Recent estimates are that about 1,300 can be detected in beer.

We possess two slightly different senses of smell. One, the orthonasal, is right where we expect it, at the top of the nasal cavity. Responding to molecules coming in through the nostrils, it is a bit more analytical and helps identify the smells we encounter. A second type, called retronasal, is a little further back in the head and responds more strongly to aromas coming up through the back of the throat; it is wired to the brain differently to be more involved in familiarity and preference. Retronasal impressions also tend to be perceived more as flavors than as aromas. Flavor itself is an imprecisely defined perception that is a bit more complex and multidimensional than either taste or aroma alone. The brain produces flavors from a mix of taste, aroma, and perhaps even mouthfeel sensations.

These two olfactory centers connect to some very ancient and primitive parts of our brains, deep inside our heads and far from the cerebral cortex, where actual thinking and language occur. These primitive parts of the brain are involved in emotion, memory, and other noncognitive processes. As a

**HEARING:**
While we don't exactly listen to our beer, noise can actually affect the way we perceive aroma.

# THE 5½ SENSES OF BEER

**SMELL:**
Beer has more than 1,000 different possible aromas, far more than wine.

**FLAVOR:**
It's not a sense, per se, but an impression created by the brain from aroma, taste, and other sensory input.

**VISION:**
Color, clarity, and the appearance of the foam say a lot about beer, but don't rely too heavily on your eyes, as they can deceive you.

**TASTE:**
In beer, sweetness, acidity, and bitterness are especially important.

**TOUCH:**
Mouthfeel is a special type of touch sensation, and you can taste creaminess, astringency, carbonation, and more.

consequence, we perceive aromas not as objective observers, but as subjective individuals, with perceptions filtered through emotions and memories created by our life experiences.

Everyone struggles with tasting vocabulary. Our brain is very good at creating and recalling emotions based on aromas, but as that sense is only indirectly connected to higher cognitive centers, the brain does a terrible job of turning aroma into vocabulary. It's just not built that way. There are tricks to make the most of our emotional memory when we're tasting. Since aroma often triggers very specific memories, you can sometimes linger and tease out what the aroma memory is all about and the place it takes you to. If you linger in those memories, they often help you identify a specific aroma — candy, perfume, cookies, smoke — that can be matched to the beer in front of you.

In addition to taste and aroma, trigeminal sensations give us information about textures such as mouthfeel, body, carbonation, and astringency. These can help determine whether a beer is correct to its style or even pleasurable. A beer's body is largely determined by its protein structure, a loose network forming what scientists call a colloidal state, which in beer is really just a more dilute version of what happens in gelatin, trapping water and creating a viscous texture. In addition, some gummy carbohydrates called glucans and other similar substances add the same slippery/creamy quality to beer as what's found in a bowl of oatmeal, where they're also present. Rye, unmalted barley, and certain other grains besides oats can add the same texture. Astringency is always a negative in beer, a result of tannins (polyphenols) that may have leached from barley or hops and perhaps were exacerbated by the brewing processes.

Vision creates expectations, which can be a good or bad thing depending on the context. We are so dependent on vision that we easily fool ourselves, even ignoring contradictory evidence from other senses to fit what we see. A beautiful beer with a gorgeous head, shimmering in a great glass, will flat-out taste better simply because we expect it to. Embellishments like brand names create the same sort of reality-twisting expectations, which is why beer is delivered in beautiful and entertaining packaging and competitions are normally conducted blind.

# THE ACT OF TASTING

**S**EASONED TASTERS have a method that takes advantage of their senses and the behavior of the beer itself to extract the maximum information from every sip.

Start with a quiet and well-lit location, free of distracting aromas. Beer is best appreciated in glassware that has a bit of an incurved rim, as this holds and concentrates aroma. It is also advisable to fill the tasting glass less than half full in order to have a place for those aromas to collect. Finally, try to serve beer at an appropriate temperature, perhaps from 38° to 42°F (3° to 6°C) for lagers and a few degrees warmer for ales. No beer worthy of serious tasting is meant to be served ice-cold.

Aroma always comes first. Different aromatics come out of the beer over time, so some may be perceptible only for a minute or so, then will waft away forever. Take small sniffs rather than deep inhalations. Think about what pops into your mind and try not to censor yourself. If the smell triggers a memory, try to tease out what your tasting brain is trying to tell you. Also, make some kind of qualitative judgment. Is it pleasant? Appropriate? Harmonious? Is there anything out of place or even unpleasant?

Then, take a sip. What's your first impression? It's likely to be a bit of sweetness, perhaps some acidity if that's present, and the prickle of carbonation. Don't be too quick to swallow. Let the beer warm up a little on the floor of your mouth. As it warms, more aroma and flavor will be released. After a few seconds, note what's happening. Bitterness will start to build as sweetness declines, shifting the balance. As you slowly swallow, close your lips and exhale gently through your nose. This should produce that retronasal sensation. Again, note any thoughts or impressions. At the end of the taste, do you notice anything harsh or unpleasant, especially astringency? The finish and aftertaste should always be pleasant and clean. Now that it's over, think about the entire taste over the past minute or so. Are all the parts good? Does the flavor pay off what the aroma promised? Are the flavors balanced and working together in a pleasing way? Is the beer what it purports to be? Then, finally, the important question: Do you like this beer?

# A WORLD OF STYLES

**B**EER AS WE KNOW IT evolved in different parts of Europe following four main traditions: British ales, Belgian ales, German top-fermenting ales (including wheat beers), and Bavarian (German/Austrian) lagers. While the history is quite complex, these four interconnected traditions are the starting point for any study of beer from a stylistic perspective. Lagers were brought to the New World by German and Austrian immigrants, and the style evolved into its own unique tradition, forming the basis for most of the world's mass-market beers. These four traditions have also been the basis for enthusiastic reinvention by an American craft beer movement that has now gone global, so things are evolving rapidly. Here's a brief description of these four great style traditions, each forged by a mix of available raw materials, climatic conditions, tax laws, water chemistry, gastronomic traditions, whim, necessity, geopolitics, and much more.

## BRITISH TRADITIONS

Beer in the British Isles was well established long before the Romans arrived in 54 BCE. In the medieval period, as in the rest of Europe, unhopped, top-fermented ales were the norm. Britain was the last region in Europe to convert to hopped beer, over the course of the fifteenth century, most experts say. It was not a homegrown invention but arrived with Flemish immigrants who brought an entire brewing tradition with them, including the word *beer*.

Gradually, English drinkers developed a taste for bitter beers, and the unhopped ales died out altogether. Strong, hoppy, amber-colored beers called October beers came into fashion, brewed most famously on private estates, and they were always described as being of very high quality. Modern styles started to evolve with industrialization in the early eighteenth century. A dark brown ale called porter and its many variants, including stout, became hugely popular in the rapidly expanding London in the eighteenth century; by 1800, porter dominated the home marketplace and was widely exported as well.

A strong distinction was made between beers brewed for immediate consumption, called running or mild ales, and those destined for a year or more of aging, during which time they developed a desirable vinous — but not sour — character referred to as "stale." In general, the aged beers were stronger and more highly hopped than the mild ones.

Around the beginning of the nineteenth century, there was a surge in the popularity of the October beers, which started to be referred to as pale ales. Over the next few decades, they became associated with their shipment to India and took on the name India ale or India pale ale. A gradual

The prized October beer was once drunk toast-by-toast from small "dwarf ale" glasses.

shift created a separate style apart from the old October beers — paler, drier, and a bit lower in alcohol. As the nineteenth century progressed, there was a good deal of interest in the more drinkable, lower-cost mild beers, and they began to dominate. A dark, light-bodied vestige of porter became known as dark mild, and this would become the main beer in England in the first half of the twentieth century. A lighter, mild form of pale ale, increasingly called bitter, was also popular.

Due to the extreme deprivations during WWI and the existence of prohibitionist groups similar to those in America, British beers dropped a couple of alcohol percentage points around that time, and they have never really bounced back. The die was cast for English beer as we know it by about 1920. Much of it was served in the form of real ale, naturally carbonated in the casks, with the final stages of fermentation and conditioning being handled by the pub's cellarman. This results in a lightly carbonated, living product that, when done right, offers a sublime drinking experience. Unfortunately, it takes a lot of care and knowledge to get it right, and the beer, once tapped, starts to go flat and sour within a couple of days.

Starting in the late 1960s, the British brewing industry attempted to switch to force-carbonated kegs and even bulk-delivered cellar tanks. There was an uproar among purists, and an organization called the Campaign for Real Ale (CAMRA) was formed in 1971 to protect traditional cask-served real ale. It failed to stop keg beer and lager from dominating the marketplace but did manage to save its beloved real ale, if only as a specialty beer, holding on to something like 15 percent of the UK market.

Scotland's brewing tradition largely parallels England's. While

A soulfully roasty stout in an Irish glass

the story is often told that the cooler temperatures up north and a dearth of hops led to smooth, dark, and malty beers, there is little evidence to support this. While there is a range of traditional Scottish ales that are a bit darker and maltier than those in England, for the most part you'll have to hunt them down. English-style bitters, pale ales, and international-style lagers dominate the market. There is a famed strong, sweet beer known particularly as Scotch ale that is a Scottish-brewed interpretation of an earlier English product called Burton ale. Ireland took a liking to porter early on and ever since has defined itself as *the* nation of stout.

On the continent, an unhopped ale called gruitbier was universal in medieval times. Spiced with secret ingredients, it was heavily taxed, usually to the benefit of some ecclesiastical organization. By 1000, hopped beer started to appear in North Coast cities like Bremen. It steadily advanced, to Hamburg, Amsterdam, and then Flanders by 1300 or so, finally jumping the Channel to England around 1400.

In addition to malt, both wheat and oats were used in beer, although because of its value in baking, the use of wheat in brewing was

**Yarrow, juniper berries, and ground ivy – some of the ingredients used in gruitbier**

frequently restricted. What these early beers tasted like is unknown, but there appears to have been a variety of them, with each town or region producing its own specialties. In those days, most beers were brewed in two strengths: a low-alcohol beer brewed year-round for quick, everyday consumption, and a full-strength winter-brewed version for serious drinking. Stronger specialty beers also existed.

**Oats were once widely used for short-lived session beers but can be useful for adding creamy texture to modern beers.**

## BAVARIAN LAGERS

It is believed that in Bavaria, the desire to brew a lighter beer year round led to the development of uniquely cold-tolerant yeast and a style of beer called lager, from the German word meaning "to store," indicating an extended aging period. The history is a little fuzzy, but this may have happened as early as 1500. At cool temperatures, yeast produces very little flavor, so most lagers emphasize the flavors of the malt and hops, on top of a smooth, clean palate.

Prior to 1840 or so, most of the Bavarian lagers would have been dark, or "red," beers. By the middle of the nineteenth century, Continental brewers were starting to adopt the more advanced English malt kilning technology, allowing them to produce paler beers. A revolutionary golden-colored beer called pilsner was born in Bohemia in 1842 and was immediately a smash hit. Similar beers appeared in Germany a decade or two later. A pale orange-ish amber beer was developed in Vienna at about the same time; it would soon become associated with Munich's famous Oktoberfest. Stronger amber-colored beers were known as bocks, and these were traditionally associated with spring.

Bavarian lager became a juggernaut that rolled over many earlier traditions, but some specialized ales persist to this day, most notably in the Rhine cities of Düsseldorf and Köln, with altbier and Kölsch, respectively. Berlin has long been famous for a sour and lactic wheat beer called Berliner Weisse, and a number of related styles existed in nearby towns. Some of these specialized beers, extinct for many decades, are starting to be given new life by dedicated brewers.

Even in lager-drenched Bavaria, top-fermenting beers survived — in the form of wheat ales known as weizens. Originally a perquisite of the royal Bavarian court, the style was privatized in the 1830s and remains popular today. It is most often served with yeast in the bottle, and this style is called hefeweizen.

## BELGIUM'S UNIQUE BEER

Belgium, a small nation squeezed between larger militaristic empires, has managed to preserve an idiosyncratic beer tradition that draws admiration from all serious beer enthusiasts. While pilsner may have the lion's share of today's beer marketplace, Belgium still retains its galaxy of unique styles, some with very ancient roots. The most historic of all Belgian beers are wheat beers such as the milky, spiced witbier (white beer) style, and its wildly sour cousin lambic, both based on the same brewing process but with radically differing fermentation regimes.

Belgium is notable today for many high-alcohol beers, an emphasis on malty rather than hoppy flavors, the use of sugar to lighten the body, and above all a huge variety of very characterful yeast strains. Belgian brewers consider their beers art in a way that's different from their European neighbors, and the result is that Belgian beers display wildly differing and highly creative and personal points of view.

Beers with a strong religious theme are common, with some even being brewed by Trappist monasteries, but these are modern in origin. Whatever monastic brewing tradition existed in Belgium prior to 1789 ended when the French Revolution shut down all monastic institutions at that time. None reopened until the 1830s, and very little brewing was done until about 1900. The beers we know today as abbey or Trappist began appearing in the 1920s and 1930s. Counter to our expectations, these Belgian styles are more derived from bocks, Scotch ales, and pilsners than from anything from Belgium's monastic past.

**Monastic institutions in Belgium and elsewhere have long brewing histories.**

Since the Belgians see the brewmaster as an artist above all else, a very personal point of view is usually present, and as a result many beers don't fit within the restrictive guidelines assigned to specific styles. While there are a few well-defined Belgian styles such as abbey dubbels and tripels, witbier, lambic, and saison, a good portion of beers brewed there intentionally shun specific style guidelines as restrictive and unoriginal.

## AMERICAN BREWING

In the United States, Germans and other central Europeans with beer traditions began pouring into the country around 1840. Prior to their arrival, the United States was not much of a beer-drinking country. Agricultural limitations and difficult travel in the vast spaces favored a more portable potable, in the form of spirits such as rum and whiskey.

For the nineteenth-century German immigrants, beer culture was an indispensible part of life, and they began setting up shop, brewing beer and establishing saloons and beer gardens in which to enjoy it. At first they brewed the beers they knew from home: malty Münchners, dark Köstritzers and Kulmbachers.

But it became obvious after a while that these calorie-laden beers didn't fit either the meat-rich diet or the steamier climate of the Americas. American-grown barley, with its high protein content, was also a problem, creating hazy beer with a sharp, grainy taste.

These problems were all solved with the gradual popularization of American adjunct-based pale lagers, brewed with the addition of about 25 percent rice or corn, which lightened the body and diluted the protein. Being crisper and more refreshing, they also suited the climate better. Lawnmower beer was born. Over the next hundred years this type of beer, eventually in the hands of just a few giant conglomerates, would come to dominate not only the United States, but most of the rest of the world as well.

By the 1970s, the number of American breweries had shrunk from about 3,500 in 1875 to well under 100, virtually all producing similar adjunct lagers that even their own customers couldn't tell apart. Inspired by experiences with beer culture in Europe, young Americans began home-brewing their own offbeat versions of classic pale ales, stouts, porters, and many more. When they started to

A GROUP OF THE PRINCIPAL BUILDINGS
ANHEUSER-BUSCH BREWING PLANT
ST. LOUIS

go commercial, craft brewing was born. By 2013, there were more than 3,000 American breweries, with a huge number more around the corner. Market share by dollars currently approaches 50 percent in craft-hot regions like Seattle and Portland. After decades as a lifeless sea of mass-market adjunct pilsners, the United States has become a real beer paradise. The excitement of this movement has spread to many other countries, and they are catching up fast.

While this is just a brief introduction to help set the stage for your further exploration, it's important to note that each grand tradition has a wide variety of specific styles and also of beers that live between or outside of standard style guidelines. For more specifics on the way styles are defined for competition purposes, you can access the homebrewing BJCP (Beer Judge Certification Program) style guidelines or the Brewers Association World Beer Cup and Great American Beer Festival guidelines for free online. Just be aware that such guidelines represent a snapshot in time and necessarily draw hard and fast lines when in some cases there really aren't any, and so they do not necessarily reflect the diversity and historic variability of these style traditions. And, of course, some brewers scoff at style guidelines altogether, so it is always wise to look outside the boundaries.

# A DICTIONARY OF COMMON BEER STYLES

**Altbier** A hoppy, dry, and brown top-fermenting beer from Düsseldorf, Germany.

**Amber Ale** A broad term that refers to some historical beers but usually describes a non-hoppy American craft beer of middling strength.

**Amber Ale**

## American Adjunct Lager
Originated in the United States, but it is now the characteristic style of most of the industrial lager around the world — yellow, fizzy, light-bodied, and minimally hopped. Uses corn, rice, or sugar to lighten body and improve drinkability.

## APA (American Pale Ale)
The exuberant reinterpretation of the English style created in the late 1970s by American craft brewers. Typically features the resin plus citrus plus floral character of Cascade and related hops and the burnt raisin notes of caramel malt, but many variations are possible.

**Baltic Porter** A surviving remnant of the once mighty porter style, now usually brewed as a smooth, cappuccino-like dark lager with a soft chocolate finish.

**Berliner Weisse** Berlin's famous low-gravity wheat beer soured by lactic bacterial fermentation, usually served with a fruit or herb syrup.

**Bitter** A range of English pale ales from golden to amber, usually hop-focused and light in body. At the higher end of its strength range, it is synonymous with pale ale.

**Bock** A strong lager, typically amber to deep golden, although dark versions exist.

**Brown Ale**

**Doppelbock**

**Brown Ale** A very broad term, but applied to a specific light-bodied English style associated with the north of the country. Craft-brewed versions in the United States are usually darker, stronger, and hoppier.

**Burton Ale** A dark, strong, and somewhat syrupy specialty of Burton-on-Trent before it became famous for India pale ale.

**Cascadian Dark Ale** A recently developed style of IPA in which black malt coloring is used to give a deep chestnut hue without a great deal of roasted character, topped off by the requisite Northwest hops. Also called black IPA.

**Cream Ale** A once-popular style in the form of a golden ale with some

adjunct content, brewed by U.S. lager breweries in a regional belt from Boston to Cincinnati.

**Doppelbock** Stronger version of bock, most often brown, but sometimes golden or amber.

**Dortmund Export** A golden lager with a very even balance and a unique minerality attributed to the oddball local water, and about 1 percent higher in alcohol than pilsner or other everyday lagers. *Export* is used in Germany to describe any strongish pale lager.

**Dubbel** Middle of the abbey beer range, usually deep amber to light brown, with cookie or raisiny malt character and spicy/fruity Belgian yeast character. Sugar is used to lighten the body and improve drinkability.

**Gueuze**

**Eisbier, Eisbock** A rare specialty lager in which water is removed during a freezing process, concentrating alcohol, residual sugars, and everything else.

**ESB** The strongest subcategory of bitter, extra special bitter is used as a trade term by a few English brewers. When brewed in the United States, it is almost always a darker, malt-focused interpretation.

**Export** A general term applied to beers that are brewed a bit stronger and often hoppier to better withstand travel and make the cost and effort involved in exportation worthwhile by supporting a higher price. Properly applied to German pale lagers, and especially associated with the balanced historical lager of Dortmund.

**Flanders Red and Brown Ales** A family of closely related partly soured ales from Belgium. A portion of beer that has been aged for up to two years in oak vats is blended with a fresh version for a unique sweet-and-sour flavor profile with lots of complex fruity and other aromas.

**Framboise** A version of lambic or gueuze with raspberries added.

**Gueuze** A popular bottled and highly carbonated blend of lambics of differing ages, taking at least two years to create.

**Hefeweizen, Hefe Weizen** Bavarian wheat ale with up to 70 percent malted wheat and a unique yeast that produces a banana/bubble gum/clove aroma profile. Very creamy and highly carbonated, and served with yeast (**hefe**) in the bottle.

**Ice Beer** A strong American adjunct lager, made in a similar manner as light beer, but to a higher gravity, frozen, the ice filtered out, and then water added back to satisfy the U.S. government's ban on concentrating effects, which it views as distillation.

**Imperial Stout** A term derived from the practice of shipping staggeringly strong stouts to the court of Russia in the eighteenth and early nineteenth centuries. *Imperial* is also a broad term that has long been applied to strong, special, or otherwise luxurious editions of standard beer styles.

**India Pale Ale, IPA** A pale, strongish, and always hop-centric member of the English pale ale family. U.S. versions tend to be stronger and much more aggressively hopped, with American-character hops displaying floral, citrus, resin, and other pungent characteristics.

**Irish Dry Stout** A uniquely Irish style exemplified by Guinness, with a light body, creamy texture, and sharp, coffee-like roast character from black roasted barley rather than black malt. It comes in a variety of strengths, but the low-alcohol draft version is the most widespread.

**Kölsch** Pale golden top-fermenting beer produced in the city of Köln (Cologne) on the Rhine River, but also brewed in the United States and elsewhere. It is considered a hybrid beer, top-fermented, but with an extended cold conditioning, much like a lager. Mainly all-malt, but wheat is sometimes used to improve the head.

**Kriek** A version of lambic or gueuze with cherries added during aging.

**Lambic** An appellation incorporating a family of wild-fermented beers native to Payottenland, an area that encompasses southeast Brussels and the suburbs beyond. Lambics feature an unusual turbid mash, spontaneous fermentation in oak barrels, extended aging, blending, and many other unusual characteristics. Substyles include gueuze

**Kölsch**

(a carbonated blend) and faro (a blend of lambic and small beer, often colored and spiced) and fruited versions called kriek (with cherries), framboise (with raspberries), and others.

**Light Beer** An American-style adjunct beer with reduced alcohol and calories, made possible by the use of industrial fungus-derived enzymes that break all available carbohydrates into fermentable sugars.

**Maibock** A golden to pale amber bock, or strong lager, originally associated with the month of May (*Mai*). Hopping is moderate but definitely more pronounced than in darker bocks.

**Malt Liquor** A deranged variation on American adjunct lagers, usually boosted to high alcohol levels by the use of sugar and targeted at minorities and low-income markets. Sometimes brewed and marketed with tongue in cheek by U.S. craft brewers.

**Maibock**

**Märzen** A style of lager that originated as a strongish beer brewed in March and lagered over the summer. Became connected with the malty amber Vienna lager style, of which Märzen is a slightly stronger variant. Long the main beer associated with Oktoberfest, but now public taste is turning to paler, crisper export beers for that festival.

**Mild Ale** Once a general term in England indicating a beer brewed for quick consumption, *mild* came to most often mean a dark, low-gravity style that was very popular in England in the first half of the twentieth century.

**Oktoberfest** A style of lager associated with the famous festival, and an appellation owned by the brewers of Munich. Once synonymous with Märzen, over the past decade or so the style has lightened in color and body and it now bears little resemblance except for slightly elevated alcohol content, and as such is sometimes now described as an export beer.

**Old Ale** A type of British strong ale that has undergone an extended aging in oak, picking up complex and often slightly wild flavors during the process. Also applies to similar beers that are a blend of new beer with some aged, for a less intense experience.

**Red Ale**

**Ordinary** A term for the lightest tier of British bitter.

**Pale Ale** A broad category of amber to golden English ales that encompasses the bitter style (see page 46).

**Pilsner** The original pale lager, first brewed in Plzen, Bohemia, in 1842. Golden-colored, all-malt, and with a robust bitterness from very high-quality hops.

**Pils** Synonymous with pilsner, but the name is usually applied specifically to German versions, which tend to be paler and drier than the Bohemian originals.

**Porter** Broad category of dark British ales that once included stout among its variations. Usually somewhat paler in color than modern stouts, but there is no clear demarcation.

**Red Ale** A vague term covering almost any variation on a deeply amber beer, increasingly applied to a type of craft-brewed hoppy pale ale with a reddish-amber hue and burnt sugar or caramelized raisin notes from the dark caramel malts used. Often adulterated — pleasantly — with rye.

**Saison** A pale, moderately strong golden Belgian beer fermented with yeasts that add distinctive pepper and allspice aromatic notes. May be fairly hoppy by Belgian standards.

**Schwarzbier** A dark lager with a soft, roasty character, associated with Kulmbach, Köstritz, and Andechs, in Germany, but also brewed in Japan as a specialty beer.

**Scotch Ale** A strong, dark, sweet, and malty beer sometimes known as a wee heavy.

**Schwarzbier**

**Tripel**

Because of their very high carbonation levels, Belgian tripels and other strong ales should be served in glasses with a lot of extra headroom.

**Steam Beer** A historical style using lager yeast at room temperatures, creating a sort of hybrid ale. It was popular in the mid- to late nineteenth century on the American West Coast, where ice for cooling was hard to get, and it is especially associated with California. Anchor Brewing Company's Anchor Steam beer, while legendary, was created from the ground up in 1971 and bears only passing resemblance to its historical predecessors.

**Stout** A term originally just meaning "strong," but eventually applied to a British black beer, brewed in several strengths and substyles. Most enduringly brewed in Ireland, but popular as a specialty beer in many parts of the world.

**Strong Ale** A rather broad term for stronger English ales, often dark in color, that have been produced without extended aging. May be synonymous with winter warmers or English barley-wines, which tend to be lighter than their American counterparts.

**Tripel** Dutch word for "triple," applied to a strong, pale golden abbey-style ale. Typically sugar is added to lighten the body and make it more drinkable.

**Weizenbock** A strong and often dark version of Bavarian hefeweizen, usually displaying rich, cookie-like flavors with plenty of fruit and spice aromas.

**White Ale** See witbier.

**Winter Warmer** Seasonal beer in the English tradition. Typically dark, with moderate to high hoppiness and a certain amount of toastiness.

**Witbier** Unique hazy spiced wheat or "white" beer associated with the Belgian towns of Leuven and Hoegaarden. A high proportion of raw wheat and a little oats lend a luxuriously creamy texture, while coriander and orange peel add a bright spiciness.

# SERVING, POURING, GLASSWARE, AND STORING

**T**HE PRESENTATION of beer deeply affects our enjoyment of it, so it's worth a little effort to get this right. A lot of the already discussed information about distractions, serving temperatures, and having the proper expectations applies here as well.

There is a lot of mumbo-jumbo out there regarding beer glasses, and there is a lack of any real science. I do think that for critical tastings, a curved vessel like a wineglass is hard to beat, and of course there are beer-specific glasses that share this feature. It's also a good idea to pay attention to traditional glasses associated with specific styles, such as the elegant footed flute used for pilsners.

It makes sense to serve beer in portions related to its strength — nobody needs a pint of barleywine.

## BEER STRENGTH, SERVING SIZE, AND ALCOHOL

APPROXIMATE NUMBERS OF "STANDARD" SERVINGS* BY SERVING SIZE AND ALCOHOL %
*Based on "standard" serving of one 12-ounce beer at 5% ABV

LITERS ▶    .2 L     .3 L     .4 L     .5 L     .6 L

ALCOHOL — % by Volume

| ALCOHOL | 6 | 8 | 10 | 12 | 14 | 16 | 18 | 20 |
|---|---|---|---|---|---|---|---|---|
| 12 | 1.2 | 1.5 | 1.7 | 2 | 2.3 | 2.6 | 2.7 | 2.9 |
| 11 | 1.1 | 1.4 | 1.6 | 1.9 | 2.2 | 2.3 | 2.6 | 2.8 |
| 10 | 1 | 1.2 | 1.5 | 1.7 | 1.9 | 2.2 | 2.4 | 2.7 |
| 9 | 0.9 | 1.1 | 1.3 | 1.6 | 1.8 | 2.1 | 2.3 | 2.5 |
| 8 | 0.9 | 0.9 | 1.2 | 1.4 | 1.6 | 1.9 | 2.1 | 2.4 |
| 7 | 0.6 | 0.8 | 1.1 | 1.2 | 1.5 | 1.8 | 2 | 2.2 |
| 6 | 0.4 | 0.7 | 0.9 | 1.1 | 1.3 | 1.6 | 1.8 | 2.1 |
| 5 | 0.3 | 0.5 | 0.8 | 1 | 1.2 | 1.5 | 1.7 | 1.9 |
| 4 | 0.1 | 0.4 | 0.7 | 0.9 | 1.1 | 1.3 | 1.6 | 1.8 |

FLUID OUNCES

Session beers such as European lagers and English bitters are often served in large glasses of about a half-liter. It's a simple calculation to figure how much beer of any given alcoholic strength will equal a standard drink serving, usually figured at 14 grams or 17.7 milliliters (0.6 ounces) of pure alcohol.

What constitutes a proper pour varies from place to place and has undoubtedly been the cause of fistfights, as people tend to feel passionate about their beer and how it's presented. While there may be arguments over a beer's head, most of us enjoy the appearance and texture as long it doesn't rob space in the glass that might be better filled with beer. For that reason, glasses for highly carbonated beers such as weissbiers and Belgian ales often have an oversized headspace as an accommodation.

There is a tradeoff between the density of the head and the time it takes to pour it properly. In the impatient United States, beers are normally poured without a lot of fuss, resulting in a perfunctory head that collapses fairly rapidly. In the traditional lager regions of northern Europe, special taps are used that deliver a little more foam. The beers are poured, allowed to settle, and then topped off in two or more steps. This creates a dense, creamy foam with tiny bubbles that lasts a good deal longer than the American type of pour. The proper amount of foam served on a pint of real ale in England is a topic as hot as an electric eel, and I won't touch it, except to say that as you move north in that country, more head becomes the norm.

If you like a firm-foam type of pour, you can duplicate it with

bottled beer. Just pour the beer right down the center, allow it to settle, pour again, and repeat as often as necessary to fill the glass. You'll be rewarded with a rich, creamy head and, as a bonus, a beer that is relieved of some excess gas, making for a better tasting experience.

One should also be aware that draft systems need precise engineering and frequent cleaning, and that, sad to say, many serving establishments are less than diligent. Also, many tap systems in the United States are incorrectly pressurized with mixes of $CO_2$ and nitrogen rather than pure $CO_2$, resulting in less than adequate $CO_2$ pressure and thus allowing the beers to lose their carbonation within a few days.

Beer is a perishable product. With the exception of very strong beers, few are meant to age after leaving the brewery. Most normal beers change noticeably after a few months. How quickly they deteriorate depends on the beer and the storage conditions. Heat is the number one enemy, so store beer as cool as you can, and avoid repeated temperature swings. Light also deteriorates beer, transforming certain hop substances into a chemical called mercaptan, which has an unpleasant skunky aroma. In full sunlight, it takes just seconds to skunk a beer. Because skunkiness is caused by blue light, brown bottles offer fairly good protection, but green and clear bottles do not. It's not only bright sunlight that's a problem. In the wrong bottles, beer will skunk inside the store or cooler case when exposed to fluorescent lights.

# A FEW COMMON
# BEER GLASSES
## AND THEIR USES

Here are some commonly encountered glass shapes that are useful to have handy when tasting your way through a year of beer. *Note:* Glass sizes are noted with some extra room reserved for foam.

**Footed Pilsner** Great for all pale, bright beers, not just pilsners. Tapered shape supports the head.

Varies, but generally 10 to 14 ounces (300 to 410 ml).

**No-Nick and Curvy Pint** Two capacious classics for British beers. *No-nick* refers to the bulge that keeps the rims from nicking when bumped together.

Imperial pint, 20 ounces (590 ml), also available in half–imperial pint (300 ml) size.

**"Willi" Glass** A modern lager glass equally useful for light and dark beers. Incurved rim helps trap aroma.

Half-liter (17 ounces); smaller sizes may be available.

**Pokal** A short-stemmed smaller beer glass with a traditional bucket shape properly used for doppelbocks, or a modern curved profile useful for a wide variety of beers.

Sizes vary, but generally about 1/3 liter (11 ounces).

**Snifter** A stubby footed form originally meant for spirits such as brandy. Great for strong beers that need to be served in small quantities.

8 to 12 ounces (240 to 350 ml).

**Seidel/Stein** Chunky handled mugs make holding onto those big beers easier. Classic for Oktoberfest or any kind of biergarten drinking. Lidded versions keep the bugs out. "Krug" is a very similar vessel, usually made of stoneware.

Full liter or "Maß" (33 ounces) or half-liter sizes (17 ounces) available.

**Tulip** Tall footed glass interpreted in a variety of designs, but the best have a curvaceous shape that flares at the rim. As close to an all-purpose beer glass as I have found.

12 to 16 ounces (350 to 470 ml).

**Chalice** A Belgian glass with monastic connections, mostly available as brewery-specific imprinted versions. The wide bowl on a tall stem makes a dramatic presentation and reinforces the religious connection.

12 to 14 ounces (350 to 410 ml).

**Flute** Tall, elegant footed glass similar to champagne flutes or sometimes created specifically for beer. Best used for pale, elegant, strong beers, but glorious for fruit ales.

8 to 12 ounces (240 to 350 ml).

**Shaker Pint** This squat and unflattering glass was created as half of a cocktail shaker and was never meant for serving any beverage. In the United States, it is the overwhelming choice of bars because of its low cost and indestructibility, qualities that only add to its loathsomeness.

16 ounces (470 ml), but beware, some examples hold only 14 ounces (410 ml).

**Weissbier "Vase"** This ancient form highlights the luminous beauty of Bavarian hefeweizen and offers plenty of headroom. In Melbourne, Australia, a half–imperial pint version is known as a "pot."

Half-liter (17 ounces) is the classic, but other sizes are available.

**Proprietary Beer Glassware** Whether the custom glass is scientifically designed or just a whim of some marketing person, drinking any beer out of its own special glass elevates the beer experience — but note that logoed shaker pints don't count.

# A FEW WORDS ON BEER AND FOOD

**O**NE CANNOT POSSIBLY explore the glories of drinking beer with the seasons and miss out on the opportunity to enjoy it with food. In the old days, people needed little guidance. Beers and their cuisines had evolved to a harmonious state, whether in Germany, Belgium, or elsewhere. Seasonality was built into food just as it was with beer. In a more cosmopolitan world, we are faced with endless choices, so it helps to have a little guidance to improve your odds of putting together a divine combination. The Brazilians use a term — *harmonizacão*, meaning "harmonization" — that I think is an accurate and elegant way of describing the goal. The idea is to blend the partners in a way that honors both but also transforms them, ideally becoming better than either one alone. A much better term than *pairing*, I think.

It's a complex subject, at the moment with little scientific basis or even broad consensus on specifics, but most agree that anyone considering working with beer and food should consider a few points as they ponder the possibilities.

## AVOID THE BAMBI VS. GODZILLA EFFECT

With the huge range in flavor intensities in the beer and food worlds, it's easy to come up with a combination where one partner totally overwhelms the other. There is no specific method for avoiding this, just simple common sense. Beer's intensity may be affected by gravity, alcoholic strength, sweetness, bitterness, roastiness, or fermentation. With the food partner, consider not just the main ingredient, but also the cooking method, spicing, sauce, and other items that may be on the plate.

## FIND HARMONIES IN THE AROMATIC REALM

Because beer is made from cooked grain and seasoned herbs, it offers a huge range of possible connections to almost any kind of food. Just look back through the beer vocabulary

earlier in this chapter and now think about foods instead of beer. And while it is obvious that flavors that are similar taste good together, that is not the only possible relationship. There are many great partners that have little in common: butter and bread, chocolate and coconut, caramel and nuts. Cast a wide and open-minded net when seeking successful partnerships.

## DEAL WITH CONTRASTING TONGUE TASTES

The dynamics can be a little complex, but fortunately there are a limited number of tongue tastes we need to deal with, so this is more manageable. Tastes like sweet, bitter, and fat are intense in the mouth and need to be countered and brought into balance in the pairing. Alcohol and carbonation also have important roles, especially in relation to fat, which the former dissolves and the latter literally scrubs away. So, sweetness in food can be balanced by bitterness in beer, and that can come from either hops or roasted malts. Umami behaves in much the same way. Fat can be balanced by bitterness and cleansed by alcohol and carbonation. For beers that have noticeable acidity, this acidity can act as it does in a wine pairing and cut through a fatty dish.

On the flip side, beers with big bitter or roasty flavors really need food with a lot of fat, sweetness, or umami to stand up to their intensity.

**Cheese and beer are among the easiest and most rewarding pairings, a great place to start to explore beer and food.**

Counterintuitively, similar tastes can sometimes balance each other out. Sweetness, for example, can only get so sweet, so when you put a sweet beer with a sweet dish, they tend to neutralize each other in a surprising and delicious way. Because beer always brings bitterness and carbonation, the wine rule that the drink always be sweeter than the dessert does not always apply.

**Stout with Chocolate Cake**

## IT'S NOT COMPLEMENT OR CONTRAST, BUT BOTH

Beer and food harmonizing is not a zero sum game, so it's nearly always possible to have both of these important relationships working. Tongue tastes are nearly always contrast-y, so the dynamics have to be considered. The aromatic realm offers so many possibly connecting points, it's a rare dish indeed that can't find a sympathetic beer complement.

## FAMILIARITY PAIRINGS ARE WORTH SEEKING OUT

There are some partnerships in which beer can supply a familiar flavor in an entirely new context, re-creating a familiar flavor experience that doesn't normally include beer — or any drink, for that matter. Here's an example: Put a gooey washed-rind cheese together with a toasty brown ale, and presto, you have liquid grilled cheese sandwich in your mouth. The dark beer forms the toasty component when there's no actual bread in the mix. Pair a fruity hefeweizen with a fresh buffalo mozzarella, and you have a milk and fruit explosion that resembles peaches-and-cream ice cream.

## LADDERS MAKE IT EASY TO BRANCH OUT

Like the toast and cheese example mentioned above, many combinations can work successfully at various levels of intensity, matching more intense beers with more intense foods up the flavor ladder and less intense foods on lower rungs. With the cheese pairing, you start with a beer like a British-style pale ale with just a hint of toasty crispness and put it with a mild and buttery bierkäse or Caerphilly, and you get a buttered-crackers sort of experience. Step it up and you get into various levels of the grilled cheese concept. Move up to an aged cheese like a Parmesan and you go from expanding the cheese flavors to including full-on meaty flavors. With a seriously roasty beer like a Baltic porter or an imperial stout, it transforms into a sort of liquid cheeseburger effect, the beer now supplying the grill marks on the virtual meat. Blue cheese and IPA is another well-known flavor ladder, and almost every harmonization idea works up and down in intensity at least to a certain extent.

**IPA with Blue Cheese**

## CONSIDER NATIONAL TRADITIONS

Don't forget to have a look at the way traditional beer-drinking countries put beer and food together. There is a lot to learn from these historic cuisines, and you'll often come up with some unexpected combinations. Germany, England, France — Alsace, really — and Belgium should be on your list for study.

# CHAPTER
## Spring
### THREE

**After a winter filled** with a hundred different forms of semifrozen water, the first sighting of springtime bock beer is as welcome as the first crocus punching up through the remaining few inches of slowly melting black snow. This beer above all others is associated with spring. Rich, malty, and golden to ruby in color, bock beer is the crown jewel of the lager family — fortifying, sustaining, satisfying.

THE STORY OF BOCK BEER begins with Crooked Waters, a tributary of the Ilm River, near the town of Einbeck, in central Germany. This water made the town one of the earliest international brewing centers, exporting beer as early as the eleventh century. By 1325 there was a warehouse full of Einbeck beer in Hamburg, the home base of the Hanseatic League, a trading organization that brought it to such distant ports as London, Russia, Norway, and even Jerusalem.

Early in the 1600s, a chronicler described Einbeck beer this way: "This delicious, palatable, subtle, extremely sound and wholesome beer, which because of its refreshing properties and pleasant taste is exported to faraway countries . . . all such Einbeck beer which shows the proper savor is a delicious famous, and very palatable beverage and excellent beer, wherewith a man, when partaken of in moderation, may save his health and sound senses, and yet feel jolly and stimulated."

Another source gives a little more detail: "Of all summer beers, light and hoppy barley beers, the Einbeck beer is the most famed and deserves the preference. Each third grain to this beer is wheat; hence, too, it is of all barley beers the best." Other sources add that the beer was pale and highly hopped.

Munich was a big customer, but by the mid-1500s it was starting to develop its own brewing reputation. The popularity of Einbeck beer may have stimulated Munich's brewers to create their own version, and the story goes that the Einbeck name was corrupted to *ein bock,* not a very satisfying tale.

More interesting is the fact that the German word *bock* means "male goat," as in the English word *buck*, referring to a male deer, goat, or other ungulate. This invokes the billy goat as a potent symbol of fertility, since ancient times symbolized by the astrological sign of Capricorn and firmly connected to spring, the season of rebirth. The leering goat faces on the labels and posters of old American bock beers bears out this connection. It may be just happy coincidence, but another thing the billy goat is known for is its kick, summing up the product it represents.

The mystique associated with bock beer lingers on in the old belief that somehow bock beer is made from the sludge removed from fermentation tanks during spring cleaning, which could never have been true. So, cut this out and carry it in your wallet:

NOTE: *BOCK BEER IS NOT, NOR HAS IT EVER BEEN, MADE FROM THE GUNK AT THE BOTTOM OF THE BARRELS. IT IS A STRONG LAGER BEER MADE THE ORDINARY WAY, FROM MALT, HOPS, WATER, AND YEAST. THIS COMES FROM A VERY GOOD AUTHORITY, PRINTED IN AN ACTUAL BOOK.*

Bock beer has been associated with the male goat for countless centuries.

# START YOUR
## spring bock fling with a super-intense eisbock.

Then, as now, southern German tastes preferred a sweeter, less bitter beer, and the hoppiness of bock was accordingly reduced when it moved into Bavaria. Eventually laws were introduced that specified the strength of the wort (unfermented beer). Today, by law German bock must be at least 16° Plato (1.066 OG), with an alcohol content not less than 6.6% ABV.

The Paulaner brewery in Munich lays claim to a stronger version, called doppelbock. The former monastery was converted to a prison and the beer brand privatized around 1800. About that time, Paulaner named its strong bock beer Salvator (meaning "savior"). The term quickly became generic for similar beers, but around 1900, Paulaner began to defend its trademark, and other breweries changed their beers' names but kept the -*ator* suffix, such as Imperator, Kulminator, Impulsator, and Celebrator. That tradition has been respected to the present day. By German law, doppelbock must be at least 18° Plato (1.072 OG).

You might start your spring bock fling in earliest March with a super-intense eisbock, a brew that is made by freezing the beer and removing some of the ice, thereby concentrating the alcohol and everything else. It's thick, syrupy, and delicious. When Lent comes along, it's time for fasting, but due to a loophole, somehow strong beer is not on the forbidden list, so a doppelbock can stand in for the forbidden foods. Or if you're looking for something less heady, a regular old single bock will do.

As the season warms, the heavier beers give way to paler, drier types, and by May, when the beer gardens open, you're on to the maibocks — golden in color, sweetly malty, but adequately balanced by classic noble hops, a sure sign that summer is right around the corner.

## ROUNDUP OF April EVENTS

### DARK LORD Day

This ad-hoc beer festival hosted by Three Floyds takes place the last weekend in April at a nondescript industrial park in northern Indiana, about an hour southeast of Chicago. It is mainly a release party and purchase opportunity for Dark Lord Imperial Stout, the most iconic among the current crop of highly sought-after collectors' beers. After registering online and getting your tickets, then waiting to collect your allotment of rare Pokémon cards, er, I mean Dark Lord, you can get down to the real business of the event, which is participating in tasting circles, where a bottle of something rare and cool gains you entry to taste others like it with fellow devotees. Plenty of food, music, amusements, and some of the best people watching on the planet as long as you're cool with the tipsy 'n' tatted. Serious fun, except the waiting-in-line part.

## CELEBRATE:
# KING GAMBRINUS'S BIRTHDAY, APRIL 11

While the legendary king of beer has been linked to several historical characters, sometimes with wildly entertaining stories, Gambrinus was pure sixteenth-century German fiction, mis-spelled from *Gambrivius* to the current form in a later Flemish transla-tion. So we can't really know when he was born, or where, but who cares? Sometimes it's just enjoyable to engage in a beery group hallucination.

# Beer Weeks

- **Milwaukee Beer Week (Wisconsin)**

- **Missoula Craft Beer Week (Montana)**

- **Pittsburgh Craft Beer Week (Pennsylvania)**

- **Albuquerque Beer Week (New Mexico)**

- **Tulsa Craft Beer Week (Oklahoma)**

# ZYTHOS BEER Festival

This is *the* legendary beer festival of Belgium, held in the university town of Leuven, long famous as a great drinking town and the traditional locus of the witbier style. It takes place during the last weekend of April.

# BEST BEERS WITH GRILLED LAMB

**A** **SPRINGTIME** classic, lamb is a demanding dish, with its rich fattiness and slightly gamey flavors; grilling or roasting over wood ramps up the intensity even more. Lamb cooked like this demands a substantial beer with plenty of bitterness and/or roasty flavors to stand up to its intensity. If you're not so much into lamb, these beers work equally well with a wood-fired steak or tri-tip roast.

**Black IPA** Also known as Cascadian dark ales, these are essentially IPAs colored a chestnut brown by the addition of a small amount of very dark malt, giving the crisp, dry palate and brisk hoppiness of an IPA with an overlay of a delicate espresso-like roastiness that provides a natural link to the carbonization on the surface of the lamb. Considerable bitterness in the beer slices through the fatty richness of the lamb.

**Rauch Bock** *Rauch* is simply the German word for "smoke," indicating a beer that has been brewed from malt that was kilned over a wood fire, lending touches of ham or bacon smokiness to the beer. Such beers are a shocker at first, as these are flavors we don't ordinarily experience together in a single sip, but once we are acclimated, they become ravishingly delicious. Normally based on the Märzen style, this rauchbier is the stronger bock version, which stands up

well to the intensity of roast lamb and with just enough deep toastiness to make an additional flavor connection.

**Imperial Red Ale** Often brewed with rye these days, this style offers a rich caramelized raisin or burnt sugar character, with the wild citrus and spice signature of American hops connecting to the rosemary and thyme typically used to season the lamb. There is plenty of bitterness to counterbalance the rich, meaty flavors, but not so much roastiness that it overwhelms the pink meat's delicate flavors.

**Foreign Export Stout** This is one of the stronger dry stouts, so named because its greater strength allowed it to be successfully exported from the British Isles in the days of the wooden ships. The sharp coffee-like character of the roasted barley echoes the flavor of the grill marks on the lamb, while the smooth, creamy texture and substantial bitterness cleanse the palate.

# BEERS FOR THE EASTER BASKET

**VERY ANCIENT PAGAN** ritual and its Christian derivative should be an excuse for a dedicated beer style. The name of the Christian festival of Easter is derived from Eostre, the Anglo-Saxon goddess of spring. Sadly, the Easter beer tradition is a bit feeble these days, especially in the United States. Lager drinkers have their richly delicious bock beers, of course, and they serve the purpose and have plentiful pagan connections. There are also beers specifically labeled as *Öster* beers from Germany and Austria, often in the blond export mode, just shy of bock strength. Belgian brewers make celebratory beers for the season, but in typical Belgian manner there is nothing about them that could be considered a defined style — they're just variants on the brewery's house style. Het Anker makes a special version of Gouden Carolus with their fingerprints all over it: strong, sweetish, and a little spicy.

Scandinavia has the strongest tradition of special Easter beers, not surprising for a region draped in dark winter for much of the year, just itching for something to celebrate in early springtime. Around 1900, Scandinavian lager breweries started brewing their versions of doppelbock, which eventually were designated *påskebryg* ("Easter brew") or *forårsbryg* ("spring brew"). Many modern versions continue in that tradition. But now we're living in a crafty world, so the style has fractured into a variety of strongish beers, sometimes lagers but more often ales ranging from hazy gold to deep reddish amber. Several are briskly hoppy, like Mikkeller's Hoppy Easter, which they describe as a "German-style IPA." Some contain herbs and spices: Jacobsen's Forårsbryg uses the spicy woodland herb woodruff, famous as a seasoning in May wine and as an herbal syrup for Berliner Weisse; Vendia's version incorporates elderflowers, a popular flavor up north; Det Lille uses sweet orange and a bit of star anise in theirs.

Easter beers in the North American brewing tradition existed, as old labels will verify, but there is little evidence that these were ever a distinct style. There are precious few spring-specific brews in the United States these days; the Bruery's Saison de Lente is a fine exception.

# WHAT MOTHERS REALLY WANT ON MOTHER'S DAY

My own mother was raised on chocolate and Coca-Cola. She liked a little wine but didn't discover beer until I was a published beer geek. When she did, her tastes remained with the flavors of her childhood. The more a beer tasted like chocolate, or really any kind of dessert, the better she liked it. Rather than stick my neck out and say what women want — an old Arab proverb says it is "toasted ice" — I'll just pick out a few brews I wish I could have poured for her before she passed.

## YOUNG'S DOUBLE CHOCOLATE STOUT

No actual chocolate present, but plenty of rich, dark complexity in this creamy milk stout. An everyday tipple for the sweet-toothed. 5.2% ABV.

## ROCHEFORT 10

Deep, dark, and softly chocolatey. A world-class Trappist ale brewed with lots of dark caramel syrup. 11.3% ABV.

## GOUDEN CAROLUS

Like spiced toffee, with a sweet, cake-like finish. 8.5% ABV.

## LIEFMANS CUVÉE BRUT

Just exactly like a chocolate-covered cherry. Luscious! 6% ABV.

## THE BRUERY WHITE CHOCOLATE

An astoundingly complex oak-aged golden wheat wine with cacao nibs. Will benefit from some aging. 14.75% ABV.

## GREAT DIVIDE CHOCOLATE OAK-AGED YETI IMPERIAL STOUT

Massive attack of everything dark and sweet, with vanilla and bourbon overtones — like melted chocolate ice cream. 9.5% ABV.

# ROUNDUP OF MAY EVENTS

## SAVOR
### An American Craft Beer & Food Experience

The Brewers Association hosts this lavish and upscale presentation of beer in a fine-food context, with selected breweries in a festival setting and food pairings at every table. Brewery staff is on hand so you can meet your heroes or just chat about the beers. Event locations (New York City or Washington, D.C.) and dates change to some degree, but it's usually around the second weekend of May.

## SOUTHERN CALIFORNIA
### Homebrewers Festival

Held at Lake Casitas, near the resort town of Ojai, a bit north of Los Angeles, this is the original outdoor homebrewing campfest. Grown to over 2,000 members-only attendees (you can join, you know), this event sponsored by the Southern California Homebrewers Association features the usual: beer, fun, food, homebrewing competition, presentations, live music, and plenty of easy homebrew camaraderie. Shuttles to nearby hotels are available for the camping-impaired. First weekend in May.

## CELEBRATE:
## FRED ECKHARDT'S BIRTHDAY, MAY 10

Fred Eckhardt is the distinguished, rabble-rousing beer author and homebrewing pioneer. Celebrate with friends over a cool glass of homebrew, or come out to the extravaganza that is FredFest, a charity beer event celebrating Fred in his hometown of Portland, Oregon.

## National
## HOMEBREW DAY
### and AHA Big Brew

It's not exactly a beer festival, but it is one of the more enjoyable things a beer lover can do on the first Saturday in May. Sponsored by the American Homebrewers Association, this is a national event celebrated at hundreds of different locations, including in private homes and commercial breweries. It's a great opportunity to get connected to the club in your region.

## CELEBRATE:

# AMERICAN CRAFT BEER WEEK

This is not a festival or a city-based beer week, but rather a nationwide celebration of American craft beer promoted by the Brewers Association, the trade group representing craft brewers in the United States. Check the craftbeer.com website for listings of hundreds of tastings, special events, and the synchronized toast to celebrate the new American beer freedom. It's usually the third week of May.

# Beer Weeks

- **Madison Craft Beer Week (Wisconsin)**
- **Quad Cities Craft Beer Week (Iowa/Illinois)**
- **South Shore, Cape & Islands Beer Week (Massachusetts)**
- **Seattle Beer Week (Washington)**
- **Long Island Craft Beer Week (New York)**
- **Santa Ynez Valley Beer Month (California)**
- **Frederick Beer Week (Maryland)**
- **San Antonio Beer Week (Texas)**
- **Minnesota Craft Beer Week**
- **Connecticut Beer Week**
- **Chicago Craft Beer Week (Illinois)**
- **Nevada Beer Weeks**
- **Asheville Beer Week (North Carolina)**
- **Melbourne Good Beer Week (Australia)**

# Other Fests

Maui Brewers Festival, Maui, Hawaii · Boonville Beer Festival in beautiful Anderson Valley, Mendocino County, California · Los Angeles Vegan Beer & Food Festival, West Hollywood, California · Southern California Homebrewers Festival, Lake Casitas, California · PA Flavor: A Celebration of Food & Beer, Harrisburg, Pennsylvania · Great Australasian Beer SpecTAPular, Melbourne, Australia · Beer Advocate's American Craft Beer Fest (ACBF), Boston, Massachusetts · Virginia Beer Festival, Norfolk, Virginia · California Festival of Beers, Luis Obispo, California · Copenhagen Beer Festival, Denmark · Ceský Pivní Festival, Prague, Czech Republic · The Cambridge UK Beer Festival, Great Britain · The Wien Bierfest, Vienna, Austria

# CHAPTER 4
# SUMMER

**As the old song goes,** the days of summer are: "lazy, hazy, crazy," and that does kind of sum it up in terms of the mood. Summer is pretty well understood to be *the* beer-drinking season. And are there ever opportunities! There are fests galore, idle vacations, quiet evenings, Sundays in the beer garden or on the beach, refreshment following work or play, and many more.

Not just any old beer will do. A summer beer should be flavorful but not too strong, have a certain crisp and refreshing quality, and present a lovely botanical aroma that mirrors the green landscape around us. A nice golden color, with or without a shimmering haze, seems to suit the season nicely, although there are some dark beers that can satisfy summer's demands. Fortunately, there are a number of great choices, from delicate pale lagers and blond ales to creamy hefeweizens and spicy witbiers. Summer is a great time to be alive and drinking beer.

# CLASSIC LAGER REFRESHERS

**ISTORICALLY,** summer was a time of low-gravity beers that refreshed the palate. The days were long, the work was hard, and in the heat, hydration is essential and too much alcohol is unwelcome, as it dehydrates the body and actu-ally makes you feel hotter. Historically, small beers were the original summertime quaffers. Very low in alcohol, hovering at or below 3% ABV, they have mostly been replaced by more modern beers.

European pale lagers are the most obvious choice for summer imbib-ing. Few of us have not enjoyed their simple charms beneath the shade in a verdant beer garden, pint after beautiful pint. Pilsner, centered in its namesake town in Bohemia, was the genesis. As the fad for smooth, clean, golden lagers bulldozed over Europe, the style was reinvented slightly in several different places. The Czech-Bohemian versions are still the richest and most luscious. German interpretations, called pils, are crisper and more austere, featuring the dry and herbal Hallertau hop or one of its relatives. Down in Bavaria, a softer taste prevails, so their helles cuts back the hops, presenting a more malty profile. The Poles have their own version combining the virtues of all three, with a bit of rustic charm, perhaps from the local Lublin hop, a cousin of the Saaz.

A welcoming beer garden is among the greatest of summer pleasures.

A NATIONAL DRINK

A HEALTHY DRINK

A FAMILY DRINK

A FRIENDLY DRINK

LAGER BIER

As golden lager developed into the immense juggernaut we see today, the style went global, but it became blander and less interesting along the way. You know the brands — they're the ones you see on television. The ads are often the most interesting things about them. Nonetheless, if you can get any of them fresh, they can be excellent lawnmower beers when a refreshing quality is more important than depth of flavor.

In terms of its market share, American adjunct lager is the king of all beers, no matter the season. It was created back in the middle of the nineteenth century as a way of solving some problems with the dark and heavy Bavarian beers in the changing U.S. market. When the first wave of lager brewers started arriving in America in the 1840s, they brought their familiar dunkels, kulmbachers, augsburgers, and other styles with them. Back in the Old Country, those beers had served a role as "liquid bread," offering substantial nutrition to a peasantry whose diet was not particularly rich. The food in the United States was quite the opposite and shockingly meat-centric. Then, as now, American drinkers didn't need a nutritious beer. Summer weather in the United States is in general quite a bit warmer than that in northern Europe, and a dark, sweet beer did nothing to take the sting of heat and humidity away. Because of the rich soil, the barley was different as well, with a much higher protein content, which meant that the beers were prone to throw an unsightly haze, especially when chilled.

One man threw himself into solving the problem. Anton Schwarz, a chemist originally from

Budapest, was the publisher of the *American Brewer* trade journal. Around 1855 he began writing articles about a new method of mashing that incorporated unmalted grains such as rice and corn, which needed to be handled quite differently from traditional malt in the brewing process. A little while later, a Chicagoan, J. E. Siebel, founder of the famous school that still bears his name, joined the chorus in his *Western Brewer*. Brewers took notice, and they were also encouraged by the rage for golden pilsner-type beers then sweeping Europe. A new class of premium beers was created that used about 25 percent rice or corn to lighten the body and dilute the high protein levels of

The busts of the two brewing pioneers J. E. Siebel (left) and Anton Schwarz (right) still watch over the classrooms of the Siebel Institute in Chicago.

North American barley malt. These beers were reasonably hoppy, at levels similar to European pale lagers, and were often aromatized with German or Czech noble hops.

Budweiser was one such beer. And while Adolphus Busch's company didn't invent the style, Anheuser-Busch, along with Pabst, Schlitz, and others, did much to popularize it. It's important to note that rice and corn were not originally used to save money; these new beers were expensive premium products, and at the time Busch started brewing with it, rice was actually more expensive than malt. The brewing process was also more intensive in its use of labor, time, and energy.

A properly brewed American lager should have a straw color and a white fluffy head and be absolutely free from any kind of haze. Aromas are usually lightly malty, like white bread or sometimes a hint of crackers, and ideally with a smidgen of hops as well. A bit of fruitiness is sometimes encountered, as these beers are generally brewed with somewhat warmer temperatures and shorter lagering times than their European cousins. The lager should be dry and refreshing in the mouth, with hops present mostly to provide a pleasant balance. They are not easy beers to brew; any

flaw will be on display in such a simple and delicate style. Clean flavors, plenty of fizz, and, most important, drinkability are the primary goals. The typical mainstream lager drinker in the United States drinks on average twice as many beers in a year as his or her craft beer–drinking counterpart, and the light-beer consumer doubles that number.

# THE LIGHTER SIDE OF ALE

**HILE ENGLAND** is not famous for sweltering summers, it isn't dank and rainy all the time either, so the British have had to solve the problem of what to drink in the warm season like everybody else. For much of the twentieth century, it was mainly mild ale, low-gravity, most commonly a dark ruby-brown in color, with a malty nose and a dry palate with little hop character. It wasn't designated a summer beer in any way, but its light body and low alcohol did serve well in the warmth. By the 1960s, briskly hopped bitter became the drink of England, but soon mass-market

Wychwood
WychCraft, an
English golden
bitter

lager reared its ugly head, and today it accounts for two-thirds or more of the British beer market.

Around 2000, English brewers started to experiment a bit and loosen their ultratraditionalist handcuffs, attempting to satisfy a younger and more adventurous consumer and trying to take back some of the ground lost to the lager juggernaut. Golden bitters, sometimes with summer references in their names, started to appear, along with wheat ales. Both employed traditional English brewing methods and ingredients. The golden bitters used paler malt for a golden or blond color and generally used hops at a lower rate than a standard bitter — although that varies quite a bit from brewer to brewer. The wheat ales showcased a grain that had long been an adjunct valued in Britain as a "head corn," employed to enhance the creaminess and stability of a beer's head. As with the closely related American wheat beer style, normal ale yeast is used rather than the wheat-specific strains typical in Bavaria, so you'll find pleasant fruity aromas rather than more aggressive bananas and spice. The beers present themselves as golden ales with a gauzy haze and a nice dry creaminess on the palate. Hopping is generally low.

# HYBRIDS

**HERE IS A** class of hybrid beers that combine techniques from both lager and ale traditions. As a summer beer, Kölsch is foremost among them. Known in Germany as an *Obergarung Lagerbier,* or "top-fermenting lager beer," it is a delicate golden ale, originating in the city of Köln (Cologne), on the Rhine River in western Germany. While it may have roots in an earlier wheat ale called *Keutebier,* modern Kölsch was created in the middle of the nineteenth century, when very pale kilned malt became available.

As the hybrid designation suggests, Kölsch shows characteristics of both ales and lagers: a soft fruitiness from an ale fermentation, but with a very clean, smooth palate gained from the cold conditioning known as lagering. Hopping is fairly light, with a bit for balance and just enough to notice in the aroma, but no more. Perhaps as a vestige of its medieval roots, a bit of wheat is often added as a means of improving the beer's head. *Kölsch* is a term that is strictly controlled in Germany, and only brewers of that city can use the term on their beer.

It is not designated as a summer beer and is drunk year-round; it is pretty much the only beer available in Köln. Taverns and brewpubs serve the beer in small 25-centiliter glasses: tall, paper-thin cylinders known as *stanges.* They are served from small casks set on the bar-tops and brought around to the tables on trays. The assumption is always that you will have another beer. To stop the flow, you must cover your glass with a coaster.

Today Kölsch-style beer is brewed by a number of U.S. and other craft brewers. It's a great stepping-stone to more adventurous drinking, and when done correctly, nothing can match its mix of easy-drinking qualities: smooth flavors and softly satisfying malt and hop balance.

While we're on the subject of hybrid ales, it makes sense to mention cream ale, a style for which I have a little personal nostalgia. I cut my beer-drinking teeth on the stuff during my college years in the 1970s in Cincinnati, home to several operating breweries at the time. Cream ale's origins are unclear, as is the meaning of the name, but it is related to a long-forgotten (except in Australia) style called sparkling ale that appeared in the late nineteenth century as ale brewers in the

United States and United Kingdom responded to the growing popularity of pale lagers.

Cream ales were mainly produced in a belt that extended from Boston south to Pennsylvania and as far west as Cincinnati. As ale-only breweries disappeared in America, cream ales continued to be made by lager breweries, and they may have been a way to offer one more product in a limited range. The story goes that the first ones were a blend of lager with a little of the strong "stock" ales then commonly brewed as a specialty item in the United States. I have not seen any documentation to support this, but it does make sense. Breweries have long blended streams of existing beers into mixtures that can be sold as various products, a practice still common in most larger breweries.

Eventually cream ale became almost a spitting image of Kölsch, although it was typically brewed with adjuncts such as corn. It underwent a long decline, and by the time my friends and I were happily slurping down Schoenling Little Kings at our keg parties, cream ale was nothing more than the brewery's lager at a slightly higher strength, sometimes with a dab of hop oil or even a little sugar to add a sense of richness.

Cream ale never found an audience outside the Northeast and Ohio, but in those areas it is fondly remembered as a beer that was a little different in an era when it was the best one could do in terms of exotic beer. In the past few decades, it has happily fallen into the hands of craft brewers, who are making more authentic and vigorous examples of this classic, let's hope for many summers to come.

# WIT, WEISSE, AND WEIZEN

**T**HIS IS A GRAND FAMILY of beers that has medieval roots and suits the summer season stupendously well. Wheat adds a creamy texture, a hint of bright tanginess, and a dry palate, all making for refreshing — but somehow satisfying — beers. The terminology can be confusing; see the sidebar at right for an explanation of the words you're likely to come across in this category.

The broad white beer family emerged in northern Europe around 1000 CE and was historically associated with hop trading centers like Hamburg and Nuremburg, a bit contrary to our modern images of these as beers with low hop rates and sometimes, as in the case of Belgian witbier, even with spices added.

## BERLINER WEISSE

Berliner Weisse is probably the oldest, last survivor of a family that included a number of sour, sometimes smoky beers such as gose, lichtenhainer, grätzer/grodziske, and others, all centered around the far north of Germany and Poland (Prussia until the end of WWI), where the long arm of the Bavarian beer purity law didn't reach until modern times.

Brewed with about half malted wheat and soured with *Lactobacillus*, Berliner Weisse was the everyday drink of Berliners until Bavarian lager barreled in. The beer was low in alcohol, at around 3.5% ABV, cloudy, tangy, barely hopped, and very highly carbonated, packed in heavy stoneware bottles that could handle the high pressure better than the handmade glass bottles of the mid-nineteenth century. The characteristic drinking glass was a huge, straight-sided tumbler capable of handling a liter of beer and an equal quantity of dense, rocky foam. Because of Berliner Weisse's low alcohol and sharp acidity, sweet liqueurs such as the

## TERMS

- **WIT** means "white" in Dutch/Flemish and refers to Belgian-style wheat ale or witbier, known in French as bière blanche.

- **WEISSE** is the counterpart in German for "white," most commonly used in reference to the sour Berliner type of beer, but also sometimes to the Bavarian type, as in weissbier.

- **WEIZEN** is the German word for "wheat," most often applied to the Bavarian wheat beer style.

- **HEFE** simply means "yeast," indicating an unfiltered beer served with its yeast, the most popular form of the Bavarian type.

- Various other modifiers include *dunkel* ("dark"), *steinfarbenes* ("amber"), *bock* and *doppelbock* ("strong" and "double strong") and *kristal* ("filtered").

caraway-tinged kümmel were often added at serving. Today, a raspberry (*himbeersaft*) or neon-green woodruff (*waldmeister*) syrup is usually added to soften the sharpness. Either way, it's a super-refreshing sweet-and-sour beer with a pleasantly creamy texture — an ideal summer beverage. Sadly, it's a beer in decline. Its two main producers have merged as modern consumers turn away from the old traditional products and look toward the mass-market lagers pitched at them. With luck, this venerable and delicious beer will find a way to survive in its homeland. If it doesn't, fantastic versions are now being made at craft breweries in the United States and elsewhere. The unique charms of Berliner Weisse are too good to let it become resigned to the history books.

## WITBIER

Another ancient beer, witbier is centered around Leuven and Hoegaarden, in central Belgium. Once the everyday drink of the region, by 1960 it was a dead beer, but it was fortunately revived by a man named Pierre Celis, who resuscitated and nurtured the style back to health, creating the Hoegaarden brand as he did. Due to his efforts, along with the style's innate charms, witbier has roared back and found an enthusiastic following not only in its homeland, but also around the world. Coors widened the audience with its Blue Moon brand, largely due to the tireless efforts of Keith Villa, one of its brewers who tirelessly championed the beer and helped it succeed in the marketplace. Now, even the mighty AB InBev conglomerate is chasing the trend.

Witbier traditionally uses a recipe that includes roughly equal amounts of very pale barley malt and unmalted wheat, plus a small percentage of oats. Together, this mix of malted and raw grains provides a creamy, almost milk-shake quality that forms the backbone of the beer's balance. Historical styles hovered around the 3 to 4% ABV range; modern versions are closer to 5% ABV. Hopping is very light. Classically it is a spiced beer, with coriander and bitter orange peel lending pleasant spicy and fruity notes on top of what the fruity yeast strain delivers. There should always be a small amount of pleasant, lactic acidity; historical sources usually mention witbier's acidity. Done right, witbier shows off a splendid opalescent sheen, a result of residual starches from the traditional mashing process.

Because of the difficulty of dealing with a large proportion of unmalted grains, getting the correct creamy texture, and managing the delicate balance of spices, witbier is a difficult style to brew. As a result, there are a lot of subpar witbiers out there, so one has to be choosy. Many U.S. brewers are eager to impress with aggressive spicing and may also be indifferent to the quality and character of their spices, resulting in disjointed, flat-tasting beers with odd and unwelcome flavors such as a savory celery seed aroma that obviously takes away from wit's potential wonderfulness.

Witbier is associated with a short café tumbler for serving, round at the rim, with a faceted octagonal base.

Witbier, spiced with orange peel, coriander, and maybe something secret, in its classic octagonal tumbler

## BAVARIAN HEFEWEIZEN

The third great classic wheat beer tradition is Bavarian hefeweizen. It had its heyday in the eighteenth century, when it was the monopoly of the Bavarian Royal Brewery. The exclusive right to brew with wheat had been taken by the royal family as a means of limiting the use of wheat in beer, ensuring there would be plenty available for bread making, but of course it turned out to be a financially successful concession for them as well. Wheat beer's popularity faded by the early nineteenth century, the rights were eventually returned to commoners, and in the past few decades hefeweizen has once again become a popular beer.

Malted wheat, typically between 60 and 70 percent, is used in the grist, lending a dry palate and a dense creaminess. Hopping is almost always light, although some brewers are starting to push the traditional limits with special editions. Modern versions are not soured. They also are not spiced, but the traditional yeast delivers a salvo of clove and allspice flavors as well as bubble gum and banana notes. Yeast strain selection, control of the brewing process, and above all fermentation temperature determine the final mix. Each

brewery tries to achieve a particular aromatic balance.

The older and more classic versions are more of a pale amber color, while modern versions look like cloudy pilsners; some breweries make both types. While filtered *kristal* versions are available, the vast majority of weizen drinkers prefer the unfiltered version. Darker versions are available, but I find them not so much summer beers, but more suited to chilly spring days. The stronger weizenbocks — rich, delicious, and redolent of banana bread — are best as cold-weather beers.

Although now available on draft, hefeweizen was traditionally a bottle-conditioned product. It is served in a tall, curvaceous glass sometimes referred to as a vase. There is a specific pouring ritual that is a great attention-getter in bars and restaurants, where a little bit of show business really can help sell great beer. The glass is rinsed first to reduce foaming, then inverted on top of the opened bottle. Both bottle and glass are then tilted to a not-quite-horizontal pouring position. The lip of the bottle is kept right at the liquid level, then withdrawn with a turning motion as the glass fills up. Once the glass is nearly

full, the last drops of liquid in the bottle are mingled with the remaining yeast by rolling the bottle on the table. The turbid dregs are then drizzled atop the foam in a circle, starting a cascade of yeasty haze that falls through the beer.

A slice of lemon is a controversial garnish. I am told by some German experts on the subject that a generation or more ago, the beers had more acidity; as the beers changed, the old-timers who preferred a more acidic beer added the lemon to compensate. The lemon is the subject of a lot of vitriol from the beer geek cognoscenti, but personally I'm agnostic. It definitely adds to the visual presentation and it's easy enough to remove, but if you're a purist, be sure to specify no lemon when you order.

## AMERICAN WHEAT ALE

The newcomer to the family is American wheat ale. These beers exploded in popularity in the 1990s in the Pacific Northwest with such brands as Widmer and Pyramid. Nothing more than simple, golden, unfiltered wheat-based ales with a modicum of hops, these differ from classic European wheat styles because they are fermented with a brewery's all-purpose ale yeast rather than with a specialized wheat strain. As a result, the beers have the pleasant creaminess that comes from wheat, but without the complex aromatic profile typical of most European wheat beers.

With a minimally exotic ingredient in the form of wheat and a crunchy granola haze, these beers gently led an entire generation into the open arms of craft beer. The process is still happening. Beers like Goose Island's 312 Urban Wheat ale are big sellers for their brands, offering a sense of something different without being difficult or challenging in any way, and drawing drinkers away from mass-market lagers. Progressive brands such as Three Floyd's convincingly hopped Gumball Head bring the wheat beer experience to those more accustomed to healthy doses of hops, so there are plenty of choices no matter your preference or experience level.

At once crisp and creamy, crowning whatever it touches with a glorious foamy head, wheat is a welcome addition to many beguiling summery beer styles.

Les coutumes du mariage

VÉRITABLE EXTRAIT DE VIANDE LIEBIG.

# A FEW JUNE WEDDING BEERS

It's been my great pleasure to have brewed a few wedding beers for friends over the years. As a homebrewer, it's a challenge to come up with something that suits the bride's and groom's personalities, will be enjoyed by the majority of the guests, and won't get people hammered from too much alcohol. A perfect wedding beer takes a lot of thought and effort, and it is always deeply appreciated. It's about as intimate as a gift gets. And really, do they need more stuff from Ikea?

The following are just starting points for 5-gallon batches, which any experienced homebrewer can easily turn into a full-blown recipe. If you're kegging, it's nice to bottle up a few Champagne-style bottles for the honeymoon.

## STRAWBERRY KÖLSCH

Take any standard Kölsch or golden ale recipe and brew as normal, then add 6 to 8 pounds of thawed frozen strawberries after the main fermentation. Allow them to sit in the beer for a week or so, then rack out, allow to settle clear, and package. The color and flavor fade fast, so this one should be brewed just a few weeks before the big day. 4.5 to 5.5% ABV.

## JORDAN ALMOND WIT

Almonds add an elegant touch to this delicious beer. Start with a classic witbier, but you can bump up the strength as you like. Try to lay your hands on the Aldrich almond variety from a California supplier or use European almonds, as both have a bit more of that classic marzipan aroma. Use 1 pound per 5 gallons. Toast the nuts at 350°F (177°C) for 10 to 15 minutes, until they start to develop a very light toasted aroma. Chop finely and add at the end of the boil in a hop bag. Hop lightly to avoid fighting with the delicate nut aroma. Contrary to common thinking, the nut oils will not degrade the beer's head. Shoot for an original gravity of 1.050 to 1.065 and an alcohol level between 5.5% and 6.5% ABV.

## TRIPLE DE VIN

Start with a base of purest pilsner malt, shooting for a range of 1.055 to 1.065 original gravity, and add enough wine juice concentrate to add 2 to 3% additional alcohol to get to around 8% ABV. It's best to add the grape juice toward the end of the primary fermentation. Hop lightly, perhaps with some New Zealand hops, which often have pleasantly fruity aromas. Belgian yeast will add one more layer of fruitiness. Because this one is strong, serve it in champagne flutes.

## LOVE CHILD MULTIGRAIN BAREFOOT ALE

On top of a base of pale ale malt, add 10 percent each of malted wheat and malted oats, plus 5 percent of flaked rye, and equal amounts of anything else you want to try such as spelt, wild rice, or quinoa, all of which will require precooking before use. Be sure to add a pound or so of rice hulls to add some of the filtering capacity lacking in the raw grains. A small percentage of a light- to medium-colored caramel malt will add color and some rich flavors, and a pound or two of honey added to the fermenter after a couple of days is always a welcome addition. It makes a great base for fruit beer as well. Gravity and alcohol can be whatever you like, but over 6% ABV and people get a little too happy a little too quickly. Hop according to your whims and the expectation level of the guests, being careful not to overdo it.

No matter which variation you prefer, pilsner always tastes best as close to the brewery as possible.

# CREATIVE LAWNMOWER BEERS

**T**HERE'S ABSOLUTELY nothing wrong with the classics, and most creative beers start there with good reason. The beers described in this chapter have been honed for centuries to suit the needs of the summer season. But many craft brewers see a classic as an opportunity to customize, just like hot-rodders and their cars. There are many ways to slake a summer thirst, and brewers are finding new and creative ways to solve this pestilential problem.

The main problem with lighter beers is that they can be light on flavor as well. Those of us used to the in-your-face character of craft beer demand a certain intensity, but it's a delicate balancing act to bring some of that vibe into a drinkably refreshing summer beer.

Wheat is common in summery beers because of its ability to make smaller beers taste rich and full in the mouth, and also because it doesn't bring the sweetness that barley malt does.

Hops offer another way to ramp up flavor without adding heaviness or alcohol. Their bitterness adds a crisp, refreshing quality, and their aromatic oils add complexity. Some semblance of balance is needed, as there is only so much bitterness a modestly malty beer will support. A light hand is best, along with a careful emphasis on aroma versus actual bitterness. A new class of session-worthy pale ales and India pale ales in the United States take their inspiration from Britain, where drinkability has been the norm for more than a century. Of course, the hop character of these new beers is thoroughly American.

Lager is great for clean, smooth flavors, but there is something intimidating about that ol' *Reinheitsgebot*, so there are not many brewers pushing the boundaries with lagers, but they're out there. There are also some modern craft interpretations of classic lagers worth checking out, especially from Firestone Walker (Pivo Hoppy Pils), Victory (Prima Pils), and Lagunitas (Pils). All are superbly characterful interpretations of classic German and Czech pilsners.

The family of so-called farmhouse beers with Belgian associations is another great starting point. Many, like the saisons, are already well suited to summer — if a tad strong for easy sessionability. But historically, Belgium was awash in rustic, low-gravity everyday ales, and there is a huge range of possibilities in this sphere. The phenolic brewer's yeasts with which such beers are fermented add a range of sharp, peppery aromas to the refreshing qualities of these beers. So, look for anything under about 6% ABV with the "farmhouse" designation, and you're on the right path.

Wild yeast and beer bacteria such as *Lactobacillus* offer another path to complexity. Yeasts like *Brettanomyces* can transform an ordinary beer with an exotic bouquet of barnyard and pineapple aromas and flavors, among others. One of my favorites is Bam Bière from Michigan's Jolly Pumpkin, a specialized brewery with a wide range of wood-aged and wild beers. This one is more or less a witbier with Brett added, giving the beer an aromatic complexity that belies its 4.5% ABV. Oak is a flavoring that can add a lot of depth and character, and the tannic finish it leaves in a beer adds refreshment as well

as character, but it can be intense, so it must be used carefully to avoid overpowering a delicate beer.

# IT'S FESTIVAL TIME!

**W**HILE SOME OF THE biggest fests take place in the fall, summer really is beer festival season. In major American markets, there are beer fests just about every weekend throughout the summer. They vary in size, style, and format, but experienced festgoers think some of the best are the ones organized by homebrewing clubs or brewers' guilds who are in it for the love of beer rather than quick profits.

Assuming there is great beer, every great festival should provide a comfortable venue, refuge from the weather, decent food, just the right amount of security, and limited ticket sales to prevent overcrowding. Done right, a beer festival can be an extremely pleasant way to while away a beautiful summer day. It takes a little expertise to have a great experience, however. Unlimited sampling opportunities and the blistering, dehydrating sun can be a bad combination. It's best to realize that there are hazards and to do your best to avoid them and behave in a way that lets your last taste be as enjoyable as your first.

If you're outside, exercise the usual cautions: Apply sunscreen as needed and protective gear like a hat. Drink plenty of water throughout the fest to prevent dehydration and mitigate inebriation. Treat the brewers and volunteers with respect; they've usually given up a lot of their personal time to make this happen and don't get a lot in exchange for it. Being civil and offering some words of gratitude to them are always welcome niceties.

Above all, monitor your own alcohol consumption, as this is the primary hazard. Most festivals attempt to limit consumption by pouring only small samples, but it's still easy to overindulge. Don't feel compelled to drink all of every sample you receive if you're not totally enjoying it. Dump buckets are always available, and you won't offend anybody. If you're serious about learning how to taste beer, you will spit or dump. If you don't love it, let it go and move on to the

next one. Alternating beer and water helps slow things down, and don't forget to eat before, during, and after. It's also important to engage in conversations with your fellow festgoers — it's hard to drink while your lips are flapping.

If you live in the area, think about volunteering. It's a lot of work, but the camaraderie is great and it's fantastic to be an insider rubbing shoulders with the brewers you worship. If it's a multi-session event, your work usually grants you access to the other session(s). Volunteers are rewarded in other ways as well, with T-shirts and other swag, and sometimes special appreciation parties.

# CLUBS FROM AROUND THE COUNTRY
## strut their stuff with fantastic homebrewed beers.

# ROUNDUP of June EVENTS

# AMERICAN HOMEBREWERS
## Association National Homebrewers Conference

## Philly BEER Week

This is the one that started it all, and it remains the biggest, baddest beer week of all, thanks to an incredible local beer scene and a few dedicated advocates like Tom Peters of Monk's Café and journalist Don Russell, a.k.a. **Joe Six-Pack**. Always a fun town for eating and drinking, Philadelphia is bursting at the seams with beer events over this 10-day period. This mother-of-all-beer-weeks features five full-blown beer festivals and hundreds of events. Runs from the end of May through the first week of June.

**This mid-June three-day extravaganza of beer-brewing geekdom travels around the country from year to year to better serve its constituency. Festivities include the final round of the National Homebrew Competition, lectures, socializing, a mini craft beer fest, and the totally awesome Club Night, where clubs from around the country strut their stuff with fantastic homebrewed beers, decorated booths, and silly outfits to match. It's not for everyone, but you know who you are.**

## MONDIAL DE LA BIÈRE, MONTREAL, QUEBEC, CANADA

**One of the most enjoyable events on the planet, this Francophone fest has a strong Belgian sensibility. Enjoy the city's public markets, local cheeses and charcuterie, and brewpubs, too. The event is usually early in the month.**

# Beer Weeks

- **Portland Beer Week (Oregon)**
- **Ohio Beer Week**
- **New Hampshire Craft Beer Week**
- **Knoxville Craft Beer Week (Tennessee)**
- **Nippon Craft Beer Week (Japan)**
- **Belgian Independence Week**

## BRAZILIAN NATIONAL
### Homebrewing Conference

There is a small but passionate beer and homebrewing scene in Brazil these days, and it is quite exciting to participate in it. This event features competition judging, presentations, a craft beer festival, and always plenty of good food. The event moves around, so check the website of AcervA (acerva.com.br), the national homebrewing club that hosts it. While the language of the conference is Portuguese, there are always plenty of people there who speak perfectly fine English. Drop a note to let them know you're coming; Brazilians are very social and welcoming to foreign homebrewers, especially if they are traveling with beer (hint, hint) or goodies like hard-to-find keg parts.

# Other Fests

International Great Beer Expo, Philadelphia, Pennsylvania · American Craft Beer Fest, Boston, Massachusetts · Beer Barons' World of Beer Festival, Milwaukee, Wisconsin · Firestone Walker Invitational Beer Festival, Paso Robles, California · Omaha Beer Fest, Omaha, Nebraska · BrewGrass Festival, Warren, Vermont · Colorado Brewers' Festival, Fort Collins, Colorado · Iowa Craft Brew Festival, Des Moines, Iowa · Epic Beer Festival, Denver, Colorado · Glastonwick Real Ale & Music Festival, Coombes, United Kingdom · Great Japan Beer Festival, Tokyo, Japan · Šumadija Beer Open, Kragujevac, Serbia · BeerFest Asia, Singapore

# SHANDIES, RADLERS, AND SUMMER BLENDS

**Shandy**

**I**T'S HOT. *Really* hot. You want a big wet glass of cooling refreshment, and of course you want some flavor, too, so a regular old light beer won't cut it. Alcohol just makes you hotter, so your craft faves may not do. Sounds like shandy time to me.

Beers blended with fruit juices and other nonalcoholic drinks have become popular in the United States, especially in warm-weather months, but these hybrids have been around elsewhere for decades or longer. Britain has its shandy, a classic blend of bitter and lemonade. Germany's Radler (literally, "cyclist") is attributed to an innkeeper trying to satisfy demand after a cycling event in 1922, but the term predates that by a decade or more; it is a blend of pale lager and lemon-lime soda in ratios between 4:1 and 2:1. Sometimes even cola is used as a blender, as in Düsseldorf's "diesel" blend of altbier and Coke. Some of these blends are available in packaged form ready to go, but most are pretty one-dimensional. Whip up tastier products at home.

Good fresh juice or freshly squeezed lemonade are key, and some exotic Asian or European sodas like San Pellegrino Limonata can be very nice as well. These can be blended into good-quality lagers, hefeweizens, or witbiers in varying proportions from 20 to 50 percent fruit and the remainder beer.

Watermelon
Nitwit

## Classic Shandy

Squeeze a couple of lemons into a small bowl, add a tablespoon of sugar, and stir to dissolve. Mix about one part of this with five parts of beer, and add a little soda water to taste. Hint, hint: The same process works
with regular or Key limes and grapefruit.

## Calamansi Smash

Calamansi is a small citrus fruit, popular in the Philippines, that has an intense sour tangerine flavor. While seasonally available fresh in some specialty markets, it is readily available at many Asian markets as small cans of juice drink or as small frozen packets of pure juice. Blend about 25 percent with a golden bitter or blond ale. If you need to lighten it up just a little more,

use some cold soda water. This works great with a witbier, too.

## Watermelon Nitwit

Packaged watermelon juice is hard to come by, but it's easy enough to process yourself. Just smash the fruit or remove the seeds and blend up the pulp and run through a strainer. Mix about one part watermelon juice to two parts witbier. A squirt of fresh lemon or lime juice will brighten the flavor.

## Grapefruit Eepah

Mix one part of your favorite IPA (could even be a double) with two parts of freshly squeezed grapefruit juice, adding a teaspoon or two of sugar if it seems a bit too tangy. As you hop lovers already know, hops and grapefruit are a natural combo.

**Cherry Bomb**

## Frühstuck Weisse

This tasty Bavarian classic is nothing more than orange juice mixed with hefeweizen, in a little more or less than a 1:1 ratio. Be sure to use freshly squeezed juice; the stuff in the carton just isn't the same.

## Cherry Bomb

Cherry juice can be found at European-focused grocery stores and health food stores, and it tastes great mixed with smooth dark beers such as porter or schwarzbier. Aim for a 50-50 blend, but adjust to your taste. A dash of ancho, pasilla, or mulato chile syrup (toast, grind, and soak in tequila or vodka to make a syrup) might be a nice addition if you want to spice things up.

## Mangomaniac

Puréed mango pulp is available frozen in Latin groceries. Use about a tablespoon of the pulp mixed with a Belgian-style blond ale, thinned out with a little cold soda water to taste. For a tangy treat, slice a fresh jalapeño or serrano chile into toothpick-thin slivers and arrange three or four of them around the sides of the glass.

## Tepache Pineapple

While the classic Oaxacan preparation calls for fermenting pineapple skins for several days, we'll take the shortcut here, using freshly juiced ripe pineapple (a blender or food processor works great), then running the pulp through a sieve (or not) and mixing the juice with a pale lager or blond ale.

## Tamarindo Tornado

Tamarind is a sticky acidic goop found inside the tamarind tree's pods, and it is a prized flavoring in many Asian and Latin cuisines. Especially valued for its refreshing qualities, it will do good service for us in a shandy. Mix a teaspoon or two of tamarind paste and an equal amount of raw sugar in a little soda water and stir to dissolve. This will blend nicely with many different beers, but it is especially good with a dunkel weizen. As with the other fruit pulps, dilute as needed with a little soda water. If you want to go with something super easy, tamarind soda is available at most Mexican markets, and you can just blend that with a delicate light or dark lager. A dusting of ground pasilla chile on top of any of these would be appropriate.

# BEERS
## TO SERVE TO THE
# GARDEN CLUB

### Lindemans Framboise

Spectacularly jammy, with a refreshing tanginess, this is a favorite with wine lovers, and it's always fun to see their shocked faces as they ask, "Is this beer?" Yes, Florence, it is indeed. Blend it into witbier or Prosecco and garnish with a fresh raspberry for an easy cocktail.

### Lindemans Pêche

Same trick, different pony — this one with a luscious peachiness. Equally yummy and cocktailable.

### Allagash Witbier

One of the earliest American breweries to get behind the witbier style, and still one of the best. Soft, fruity, creamy, and very elegant.

### St. Arnold Fancy Lawnmower Beer

This Houston brewery's take on a classic Kölsch is delicious and refreshing, but it's not available everywhere. Look for locally produced Kölsch — it's much better when it's made close to home.

### Duchesse de Bourgogne

A semisour brown ale from Flanders that has a tinge of softly tannic oak and might even remind the ladies of red wine.

**Even steadfast wine lovers might find a beautiful bouquet in these beers.**

ROUNDUP OF FOLY EVENTS

## CARNIVALE
### Brettanomyces & Andere Wilde Dieren Beer Festival

This is a multisite celebration that takes place at several of central Amsterdam's beer bars, focusing exclusively on wild and sour beers fermented with *Brettanomyces*, *Lactobacillus*, and other critters. Programs are mostly in Dutch, but the beers taste amazing in any language. Friday and Saturday in early July, Amsterdam, Netherlands.

## Siebel Advanced HOMEBREWING Program

Join the experts from the world's second oldest brewing school, Chicago's Siebel Institute, for a week of immersive training in amateur brewing. Late July.

## BLACK BEERS IN THE HOT SUN

On the face of it, high-gravity stout, usually known as Irish foreign extra, seems like a bad idea in the hot and sunny Caribbean, but this is a very popular style in the islands. Topping off at around 8 or 9% ABV, they do require a little self-control, as you can't pound too many of these before you're nearly comatose. But strange as it seems, they taste great in hot weather and pair nicely with the characterful and spicy food found throughout the region.

# OREGON BREWERS

**Festival** This long-running event produced by the Oregon Craft Brewers Guild showcases the best of the Pacific Northwest beers in a pleasant, grassy park right downtown. Event runs the last weekend of the month.

CELEBRATE:

## THE FEAST DAY OF ST. ARNOLD, JULY 8

Arnold of Soissons (alternatively known as Arnulf of Oldenburg) is traditionally viewed as the patron saint of hop pickers and Belgian brewers.

**St. Arnold Maastricht, the Netherlands**

# Beer Weeks

- **Oregon Craft Beer Month**

- **Queensland Beer Week (Australia)**

**Little Creatures Brewery**

# Other Fests

Square Roots Festival, Chicago, Illinois · **Vermont Brewers Festival, Burlington, Vermont** · Indiana Microbrewers Festival, Indianapolis, Indiana · **NYC Craft Beer Festival, New York, New York** · Sour & Stinky Fest, a beer and cheese event in Lancaster, Pennsylvania · **Milwaukee Brewfest, Milwaukee, Wisconsin** · BPONG: Masters of Beer Pong, Las Vegas, Nevada · **Toronto Festival of Beer, Toronto, Ontario, Canada** · Scottish Real Ale Festival, Edinburgh, Scotland · **ArtBeerFest, beer and food event, Caminha, Portugal** · Farsons Great Beer Festival, Ta' Qali, Malta · **Festival na pivoto Prilep, Republic of Macedonia** · Great Japan Beer Festival, Osaka, Japan · **Le Fête de la Bière, Felletin, France** · Pivo in Cvetje (beer and flowers), Laško, Slovenia · **Õllesummer festival, Tallinn, Estonia** · Beer Passion weekend, Antwerp, Belgium · **Tbilisi Beer Fest, Tbilisi, Republic of Georgia**

If a thriller novel is not your idea of escape, perhaps reading about beer would be more your speed. What follows is not a complete list of everything you need to become a genuine beer expert, but rather just a few choice beer books that I have found to be enjoyable, enlightening, and even inspiring over the years. I hope you do too.

**Michael Jackson's Beer Companion** This giant figure was probably more responsible for the flowering craft beer movement than anyone, even though he never brewed a drop of beer, as far as I know. His *Beer Companion* is illuminating and enthralling, dense with information, and always a joy to read. We owe it to ourselves not to forget this author, who was the first writer to have the balls to suggest that beer was worthy of serious study. He wrote many books; they're equally brilliant, so pick whichever you can get your hands on easily, and then work your way through his whole catalog.

**Let There Be Beer** Author Bob Brown was a versatile and fascinating writer who hung with the avant-garde set back in the day. He was a pal of H. L. Mencken, to whom this book is dedicated. Published in 1932, anticipating the end of Prohibition, it is a series of achingly beautiful remembrances of the author's encounters with beer as he was coming of age in Chicago and later in New York City. Luminous prose, some of the best ever written about beer, I think. A rather hard-to-find book that really deserves to be reprinted or released electronically.

**The Audacity of Hops** This recent fast-paced book by Tom Acitelli does a great job of chronicling

the rise of craft brewing from a broken-down steam brewery in San Francisco in the mid-1960s to the exploding wonderment we have today. Chapters are short but very insightful, and he talked to just about everybody in the business to get their stories directly. A very engaging read.

**A Vade Mecum for Maltworms** This is a small and curious book that offers to be "A Guide to Good Fellows. Being a Description of the Manners and Customs of the Most Eminent Publick Houses in and about the Cities of London and Westminster." Penned in the late eighteenth century, it delivers its commentary in wracked rhyme, caricaturing a string of taverns in quaint and ancient language. The author's opinion of each house ranges from admiring to searingly contemptuous. If you enjoy the sheer weirdness of trying to understand a culture from its own point of view, this book will amuse you to no end. *Maltworm*, if you hadn't figured it out, was a slang term for a beer fancier. A nineteenth-century reprint is available; numerous free downloads are available as well.

**Ambitious Brew** Unlike most of us who write about beer and its history, author Maureen Ogle is an *actual* historian, so she brings disciplined research to the fascinating story of the rise of American brewing. As a bonus, she has no particular ax to grind. The story starts with the arrival of German immigrants and continues until the present. Whether you love or hate Big Beer, everyone who wants to be well informed about beer should read this book to find out how it got to be the 800-pound gorilla it is today.

**The Oxford Companion to Beer** Edited by Garrett Oliver, this is the ultimate short-attention-span guide to beer, since it is broken into small articles like an encyclopedia, covering every possible aspect of beer, its production, and the industry surrounding it. As a result, it's a beast. Be especially careful if you balance it on your chest while you lie on the beach — its massive weight could crush you like a sand flea.

# BEER AND BARBECUE

**DO LOVE THE** fire and smoke. Cooked low and slow, barbecue is an undisputed American classic, and summer is its rightful season. With its bold, rich flavors, this presents a challenge, as the typically light and fizzy summer session beers can't take the onslaught of smoke, vinegar, sugar, spice, and pork fat.

As barbecue can range from delicate, maple-smoked chicken to Texas-style brisket bathed for an entire day in mesquite smoke, suitable beers can cover a wide range. At the delicate end, try perhaps a substantial Czech-style pilsner, Belgian-style pale ale, or English bitter. As you move up the intensity scale, hoppy red ales and IPAs can cut the richness of pulled pork; porters can also be very pleasant. With sweet-and-saucy ribs, a Belgian-style dubbel, with its malty aromas, dry palate, and copious carbonation, is a perfect match. For brisket, haul out the big guns: double IPA, Baltic porter, or Belgian strong dark ale.

And don't forget smoked beer. Its bacony goodness is available in a range of styles from helles to Märzen to bock to barrel-aged imperial stout. Naturally, they can all find partners in something luscious from the smoker.

While not technically barbecue, grilled meats such as burgers and steak are staples in the summer. Like barbecue, they combine rich meatiness, a bit of char, and some smoky nuances. Some of the paler beers such as IPAs will serve nicely, but I think a little more malt character suits such dishes better. A hoppy red rye ale is nice, as are hoppy and characterful American-style stouts and porters. If you're looking to bring a little beer flavor into the meat, a malty porter or a tangy Flanders-style red such as Rodenbach works wonders along with some salt and pepper.

**An obvious combination, but still sublime**

# NOTHING SAYS
# "I LOVE YOU, DAD,"
## LIKE BEER: A FATHER'S DAY MIXED SIX

Dads come in all sizes, shapes, and tastes, and you know yours better than I do. If Pop is a hophead or a sour freak, I'm guessing you don't need my help. This list suits a father who is curious about the passion for beer that's taking over his son's or daughter's life and wants a little taste.

### A Really Fine Pilsner

If you're in North America, skip the imports — they're all stale by the time you get them. Instead, pick a home-grown version such as Victory Prima Pils, Lagunitas Pils, or Firestone Walker Pivo Hoppy Pils. Each offers pure golden malt and fresh Euro-hop character.

### An English Pale Ale or ESB

These are just different names for the same thing, but if you're getting an American-brewed version, an ESB is likely to be a bit less hoppy. Try Fuller's ESB, Marstons Pedigree, Left Hand Sawtooth, Firestone Walker DBA (Double-Barreled Ale), or Southern Tier Harvest Ale, but there are many, many other fine choices.

### Witbier

This creamy, lightly spiced wheat brew originating in Belgium is as different as it is easy to love. My current favorite Belgian wit is St. Bernardus, formulated with the aid of witbier legend Pierre Celis. Or try Allagash for a great American version that sticks pretty close to the original.

## Belgian Strong Golden Ale or Tripel

While the style guidelines tease these strong yet easy-drinking wonders apart, there is barely a hair's breadth of difference between the two styles (tripel allows a bit more color and complexity). Duvel is the widely imitated classic, and still one of the best. Many choices: Victory Golden Monkey, North Coast Pranqster, Westmalle Tripel, Delirium Tremens, and more. Be sure to toss in the special glass if there is one.

## Brown Ale

There are many possible interpretations of this broad style. English versions tend to be light on the palate and barely hopped, with a nice toasty nose, like a slice of bread fresh from the toaster. American interpretations run the gamut from light and toasty to deeply toasty-roasty, and they may be pretty hoppy too. Try Samuel Smith Nut Brown Ale, Avery Ellie's Brown, Bell's Brown, Brooklyn Brown, Duck-Rabbit Brown Ale, and others.

## American Amber Ale

These are a bit of a throwback to the early days of craft brewing. As "Buffalo" Bill Owens put it: "We had a dark and a light, but what were we gonna call the one in the middle? Amber." The style tends to be a bit rich and caramelly, with a touch of hops for balance. Try Bell's Amber, Anderson Valley Boont Amber, Full Sail Amber, or, for just a tough of Belgian character, New Belgium Fat Tire.

## The Seattle INTER-NATIONAL Beerfest

Organizers describe this as a "high-end 3-day beer festival specializing in rare, hard-to-find, exotic beers." I believe it's the only beer festival in the world that you can ride to on a monorail. Seattle is awesome in so many ways! Three days in late August.

## GREAT BRITISH BEER Festival

"GBBF" is the largest real ale festival in Britain — or anywhere else, for that matter. Unlike most other beer festivals, beer is not handed out in small samples, but sold in pints or half pints, so you'll find yourself sharing with your mates. Volunteer help is always welcome, so if you don't mind working, you'll make new friends and get a unique perspective on the event. Takes place over five days midmonth.

## Great Taste of the MIDWEST

For a quarter of a century, the Madison Homebrewers and Tasters Guild has been hosting this festival in a beautiful shaded park on the shore of Lake Monona in Madison, Wisconsin. The focus here is mainly Midwestern breweries, but there is always a lot of variety beyond that. Smart festgoers bring lawn chairs and set up camps under the trees, trekking off to the tents to retrieve samples to taste. Second Saturday.

# Beer Weeks

- **Raleigh Beer Week (North Carolina)**
- **Silicon Valley Beer Week (California)**
- **DC Beer Week (Washington, D.C.)**
- **Santa Cruz County Beer Week (California)**
- **Virginia Craft Beer Month**

**CELEBRATE:**
## IPA DAY, AUGUST 1

**The Brewers Association sponsors this coast-to-coast celebration of all things pale and hoppy. Check your local beer-event calendars for one of the hundreds of simultaneous events in your area and geek out to the bitter, resiny glory of our favorite beer herb.**

# Other Fests

Stone Anniversary Celebration & Invitational Beer Festival, San Marcos, California · Mammoth Festival of Beers & Bluesapalooza, Mammoth Lakes, California · Bend Brewfest, Bend, Oregon · Oak Park Micro Brew Review, Oak Park, Illinois · Utah Beer Festival, Salt Lake City, Utah · Sierra BrewFest, Grass Valley, California · San Juan Brewfest, Durango, Colorado · Bières & Saveurs, Chambly, Quebec, Canada · Qingdao International Beer Festival, Qingdao, China · Massive Mine Beer Fest, Cape Town, South Africa · Fête de la Bière, Schiltigheim, France · Belgrade Beer Fest, Belgrade, Serbia · Dani Piva, Karlovac, Croatia · Giorti Biras (Beer Festival), Athens, Greece · Beer Festival Cuzco, Peru · Great Japan Beer Festival, Nagoya, Japan

CHAPTER

AUTUMN

FIVE

**As the days grow** shorter and brisker, we've about had our fill of light and breezy summer beers and begin to pine for something more substantial and rich. It's no wonder that fall, with its blazing sunsets and shimmering fall leaves, is the great season of amber-colored beers.

In agricultural terms, the harvest is the biggest moment of the year, when you tally up the fruits of your labor and find out if you have enough to ward off hunger through the long winter. For brewers, it's time to evaluate the new malt and hops to figure out how much beer you can make and of what quality. It's a heavy business, but it is a season of celebrating as well. Historically, one of the best rewards was to finally broach the casks of the strong "March" beers brewed at the end of the previous year's brewing season, which slumbered, slowly maturing for months, dangling like a carrot on a stick as a reward for getting the summer's business done.

# THE SPIRIT OF OKTOBERFEST

**THIS IS THE ICONIC** autumn celebration revolving around beer, lasting two weeks starting in mid-September and attracting more than six million drinkers who consume one-third of all Munich beer production in that short time. It began in 1810 as a beer-free wedding celebration for Crown Prince Ludwig I and Princess Theresa and quickly grew

into the debauched behemoth we know today. The numbers are staggering: 400,000 chickens, 600,000 sausages, 600,000 liters of beer, and tents that hold thousands of partygoers.

**Oktoberfest in Munich, Germany**

## NAVIGATING OKTOBERFEST

Having a great time at the world's largest beer bash shouldn't be all that difficult, but here are some tips to help you get the most out of the fest:

**The fest** is free to enter and there's plenty to see while you wander around, but if you want beer, you must have a seat in one of the tents.

**Each tent** has a different character, so check out the scene first and then pick the experience you're looking for.

**Finding** one or two open seats is usually not that difficult, but if you have a large group, consider reserving a table well in advance.

**Most beer tents** close at 10:30 PM; only Kater is open until 1 AM.

**Food is cheaper** outside the tents.

**Most locals** only go for a single session; after a couple of days, it gets old.

**Accommodations** fill up months in advance.

**As with any beer event,** pace yourself, remember to eat, and stay hydrated!

# ROUNDUP OF September EVENTS

## SAN DIEGO
### Festival of Beer

A fantastic opportunity to immerse your-self in the resinous, hop-drenched world that is the San Diego, California, beer scene. Starts around the third Friday of the month.

## BREWGRASS
### Festival
Beer and music festi-val in Asheville, North Carolina, a small town in the Great Smoky Mountains with a flourishing craft beer scene; usually the third Saturday of the month.

## THE GREAT CANADIAN BEERFEST

Victoria, British Columbia, Canada. A heavy focus on cask ales from the Pacific Northwest in a breathtaking set-ting. End of first week of September.

## BELGIAN BEER WEEKEND

Grand Place/Grote Markt, Brussels, Belgium. Held on an early weekend in September, this beerfest on the glorious main public square of Brussels features more than 400 Belgian beers.

## NORTHERN CALIFORNIA
### Homebrewers Festival

Taking place in a camping resort a bit north of Sacramento, this event is like a Boy Scout jamboree with beer and with-out all the annoying youths. Featuring food, talks, club booths, and a huge amount of most excellent homebrewed beer, the festival is a great way to immerse yourself in the unique home-brewing culture of the region. Usually the third weekend of the month.

## STOCKHOLM BEER & WHISKY FESTIVAL

I know this sounds like trouble on a stick, but if you can pace yourself, this is the premier beer event in Scandinavia. Showcasing the unique mix of brash, American-style craft beers and reinvented preindustrial local specialties, it's a unique window into the new Scandinavian beer, which is maturing into something very exciting. Two weekends spanning September and October.

# Beer Weeks

- **LA Beer Week**
  After a lot of false starts and thanks to a great homebrew scene and a few stalwart pioneers, this sprawling metropolis is finally starting to get its beer act together. Third week of the month.

- **Also:**
- **Bellingham Beer Week (Washington)**
- **Louisville Craft Beer Week (Kentucky)**
- **Florida Beer Week**

# Other Fests

The Great Atlanta Beer Fest, Atlanta, Georgia · Downtown Brew Festival, Las Vegas, Nevada · U.P. Fall Beer Fest, Marquette, Michigan · Cambridge Carnival Beer Festival, Cambridge, Massachusetts · Night of the Funk Belgian Beer Fest, Boston, Massachusetts · Fargo Beer Festival, Fargo, North Dakota · Beer Advocate's Belgian Beer Fest, Boston, Massachusetts · Oktoberfest, Munich (see page 118) · All-Ireland Craft Beer Festival, Dublin, Ireland · York Beer & Cider Festival, York, United Kingdom · Great Japan Beer Festival, Yokohama, Japan · Borefts Beer Festival, Bodegraven, Netherlands · Great Manila Beer Tasting, Pasig, Philippines · Joburg Festival of Beer, Johannesburg, South Africa · Bierfest, Durban, South Africa · Mondial de la Bière, Strasbourg, France · Fiesta de Cerveza, Malloco, Chile

The namesake beer has undergone numerous changes and is still evolving rapidly today. Originally a somewhat stronger or possibly even a powerful bock version of the dark reddish Munich style, it was lightened up in the 1840s by the combined efforts of Spaten's Gabriel Sedlmeyr and Vienna's Anton Dreher, who brought modern English kilning technology to lager brewing, producing a paler amber beer than had been the norm. This "Vienna"-style Oktoberfest beer remained the flagship of the festival until 1871, when Spaten introduced a slightly darker version based on Sedlmeyr's reinvention of Munich malt. That interpretation — caramel and sweetish, with a toasted

cookie edge — dominated until the past decade or so, when public taste turned increasingly to the paler, drier Munich helles style. Not wanting to toss in the towel on their beloved Oktoberfest beer, some Munich brewers began to produce paler versions, a style also known in Germany as export lager. It just goes to show you that even in tradition-mad Germany, public taste still trumps all.

In Europe, the Oktoberfest name is fiercely protected; only brewers within the Munich city limits can call their beers Oktoberfests. All others must say "Oktoberfest style" or "fest" beer. The restriction has never been enforced in the New World, so you'll find many Oktoberfest beers from American craft brewers.

Large and small Oktoberfest events are held around the world wherever there is an organized German community. Some of the best ones are smaller affairs put on by Germanic social organizations and feature authentic foods such as *spannferkel* (charcoal-roasted pig) alongside the smooth and malty Oktoberfest lager. Seek them out wherever you happen to be at that time of the year.

## A FEW ALTERNATE OKTOBERFESTS

### Kitchener-Waterloo Oktoberfest

Attracting up to a million visitors, this nine-day celebration in Ontario, Canada, is considered the second largest Oktoberfest in the world. The fest halls are operated by the many Germanic clubs in the region, lending an authentic Old World character to the event. Runs from the Friday before Canadian Thanksgiving (second Monday) through the Saturday after.

### Blumenau, Brazil

Located in ethnically Germanic southern Brazil, this is the third largest Oktoberfest in the world, attracting over 600,000 people who collectively down a similar number of liters of beer. Start with a *chope*, or Brazilian-style draft of lighter-than-air macrobrew such as Brahma, then seek out local craft beers such as Eisenbahn or Bierland, which offer a bit more flavor and variety. Happens mid-October, or spring in southern Brazil.

### Oktoberfest Zinzinnati

It's been a long time since the massive German immigration that made Cincinnati a hub for brewing and precision machine work, but the city still retains a sense of German identity, and this fest is one of its more obvious manifestations. Claiming to

be "the largest and most authentic" Oktoberfest in the United States, it offers the usual mix of beer, music, food, and foolishness such as the Chicken Dance. The Boston Beer Company is a sponsor, so its beer (Sam Adams) is prominently featured, but imports, local craft beers, and microbrews are also available.

**Wurst Fest, New Braunfels, Texas** Located a short distance from Austin, in Texas Hill Country, this entertaining event puts a weird Tex-Mex spin on the classic celebration with foods like wurst tacos eaten to the tunes of major international polka acts, all washed down by a very impressive selection of European lagers and Texas craft beers.

### Cannstatter Volksfest

Held in Stuttgart, this is the second largest beer festival in Germany and probably in all of Europe. It starts a week later than Oktoberfest but has a very similar character.

### More Alternate O-Fests:

Ho Chi Minh City, Vietnam; Sydney Oktoberfest, Australia; Oktoberfest Villa General Belgrano in the Córdoba Province, Argentina; Valdivia, Chile, Bierfest; Canberra Celebrates Oktoberfest and the Canberra Craft Beer & Cider Festival, Australia

# BEST BEERS TO DRINK

## WHILE WEARING LEATHER SHORTS

### Live Oak Oaktoberfest

A rich, brooding, and slightly dark version of the style from this Austin, Texas, microbrewery

### Victory Festbier

Rich and malty, but a little more craft-centric than most, meaning you can actually taste the hops in this one

### Shiner Oktoberfest

Pretty straight-ahead German-style Märzen from this Texas regional heritage brewery

### Berghoff Oktoberfest

Crisper and drier on the palate than most; a mostly modern Oktoberfest nicely balanced by a hint of hops

### Sam Adams Oktoberfest

Rich, chewy, and caramelly, with a hint of toasted cookie

### Ayinger Fest Märzen

An absolute classic from a traditional small brewery just outside the Munich city boundary

ROUNDUP OF
*October*
EVENTS

### Great AMERICAN BEER Festival

**This is the King Kong of beer festivals, something every beer lover should experience at least once. Denver, Colorado; dates change due to convention center availability. See the detailed description beginning on page 131.**

### Elysian Brewing's GREAT PUMPKIN Beer Festival

Seattle, Washington; early October; see details on page 134.

### The Dixie Cup HOMEBREW Competition and Mini Conference

Houston's Foam Rangers put on this wild and woolly homebrew weekend that features an early-morning barleywine tasting, a mini conference, a pub crawl, and the Fred Eckhardt Beer and Food Tasting. With over 1,000 entries, it's also the largest single-site homebrew competition in the world. Friday and Saturday, midmonth.

### Surly Brewing Co. DARKNESS DAY

A beer tasting and release for this famously limited-edition imperial stout. Takes place at Surly Brewing Company, Brooklyn Center, Minnesota, on a Saturday near the end of the month.

## SALONE DEL GUSTO

Not specifically a beer festival, this is a vast food and drink orgy focusing on very high-quality and mostly Italian food and drink. Sponsored by Slow Food, the international organization dedicated to preserving historic foodways and creating a sustainable future, it takes place in a giant convention center that was once a Fiat plant in the beautiful city of Torino (Turin), in the north of Italy. There are several aisles of *salumi* and cheese, one of balsamic vinegar and olive oil, plus bread, chocolate, and much more. The best part is

that you can get samples to taste of everything and it's all available for purchase. The event also includes an *enoteca* with something like 1,700 mostly Italian wines available by the glass. Oh, yes, and there's beer, too, from Italian and international craft brewers. Takes place near the end of the month only in even-numbered years; a cheese festival in nearby Bra happens in alternate years.

**Besides beer, a bounty of other goodies awaits you at Salone del Gusto in Torino, Italy.**

# Beer Weeks

- **Cleveland Beer Week** runs for 10 days starting midmonth, and it's getting to be quite a large and enjoyable beer week.
- **Also:**
- **Maryland Beer Month**
- **Detroit Beer Week (Michigan)**
- **Baltimore Beer Week (Maryland)**
- **Cleveland Beer Week (Ohio)**
- **Atlanta Beer Week (Georgia)**
- **Austin Beer Week (Texas)**

# Other Fests

Great World Beer Festival, New York, New York · Nashville Beer Festival, Nashville, Tennessee · Wet Hop Beer Festival, Yakima, Washington (see other wet hop fest listing on page 129) · Pumpkin Beer Festival, Philadelphia, Pennsylvania · Stoudt's Microfest, Adamstown, Pennsylvania · Grovetoberfest, Coconut Grove, near Miami, Florida · Louisville Brewfest, Louisville, Kentucky · Windsor Craft Beer Festival, Windsor, Ontario, Canada · Pilsner Fest, in Plzeň, the biggest festival in the Czech Republic · Bierfest, Johannesburg, South Africa · Oktoberfest, Ho Chi Minh City, Vietnam · Marco Polo German Bierfest, Hong Kong, China

# HOP HARVEST: WET- AND FRESH-HOPPED BEERS

**I**NDUSTRIALIZATION long ago obscured beer's agricultural roots. Those working in the craft sector are very eager to restore this important connection between the beer we drink and the land that brings it forth. Beers that use the freshest produce of the harvest are one tangible way of making this connection.

In most cases, we're talking about hops. In commercial production, hop cones are stripped off their vines and within a few hours are sent to drying kilns where the moisture is removed, making them stable for storage and shipment. If not dried within about 24 hours, the wet green cones will turn moldy and spoil. But if a brewer acts with proper haste, the fresh, "wet" cones can be thrown immediately into the brew, lending super-fresh hop aromas to the beer. Breweries may either arrange for rapid shipping from commercial hop-growing areas or use hops cultivated in their own backyards if they're located in an area where hops will grow and produce cones.

Special beers are also made in the fall season from very fresh hops that have gone through the normal drying process. Hops are a very delicate crop and begin to lose their aroma and bitterness as soon as they are stored, so these fresh-hopped beers will have a bright, lively flavor

Young hop picker, draped with fresh hops, in Kent, England, August 1937

that will be hard to duplicate once the hops have aged for a few months.

Sierra Nevada has been a leader in this movement, producing both northern- and southern-hemisphere versions, even absorbing a staggering airfreight bill to bring fresh New Zealand hops to their kettles in northern California. They also produce what they call an "estate" beer, borrowing a term from winemaking to indicate that all of the ingredients are grown on their own property, a rarity for breweries due to the cost and complexity of malt- and hop-processing systems.

So what about the flavor? If you're a lover of the wild, grassy, and a little out-of-control hop aromas and flavors, you'll love wet-hopped beers. If your taste runs a little more to the refined, you may prefer the flavors of a fresh-hopped beer. Either way, these special harvest ales are a great way of pointing out the agricultural connection that,

although not always obvious, is very much alive in beer and brewing.

Can't get enough? It might be worth traveling to one of the West Coast festivals featuring wet-hopped or fresh-hopped beers:

**Hood River Hops Fest, Hood River, Oregon:** A short jaunt from Portland, one of the largest single-day fests, with more than 60 beers

**Fresh-Hop Ale Festival, Yakima, Washington:** In the heart of Washington's hop-growing region in early October

**SDBG Wet-Hop Beer Festival, San Diego, California:** The local brewers guild hosts this fest over three days in mid-October

**Portland Fresh Hops Beer Festival, Portland, Oregon:** Two days in early October

Smaller fests at beer bars are popping up all over the place, so be sure to check your local listings.

### Two Brothers Brewing Company, Warrenville, Illinois

Rotating between citrus, piney, and sometimes herbal character, Heavy Handed IPA, with 5.7% ABV, is brewed in several slightly different batches, each with a specific hop variety and location. Drinkers can check the batch number on the label against the company's website to determine the type of hop in the version they're drinking.

### Deschutes Brewery, Bend, Oregon

In this annual limited edition of its 5% ABV flagship Mirror Pond Pale Ale, the brewery uses super-fresh Cascade hops that come from a single heirloom plot.

### New Belgium Brewing, Fort Collins, Colorado, and Elysian Brewing, Seattle, Washington

While New Belgium regularly produces the 7% ABV Fresh Hop IPA for its Lips of Faith series, the brewery teamed up with Elysian's Dick Cantwell to create an 8.5% ABV imperial version with a complex and subtle elegance: Trip Series Imperial Fresh Hop IPA.

### Sierra Nevada Brewing Company, Chico, California

Sierra Nevada makes a pair of harvest ales, one each from the northern and southern hemispheres. Northern Hemisphere Harvest is a mix of Cascade and Centennial; Southern Hemisphere Harvest uses New Zealand Pacifica, Motueka, and Southern Cross, although the hops change a little from year to year. Both are amber in color with a dab of caramel malt richness and 6.7% ABV.

It is currently the only U.S. brewery to make an estate ale, using malts and hops from the brewery's own property. With the classic Sierra Nevada house character, it is similar in malt profile to the harvest ales, but the estate uses a mix of fresh, not wet, estate-grown Chinook, Cascade, and Citra hops.

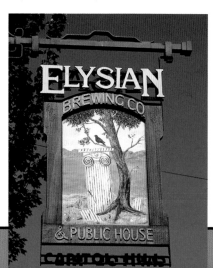

# THE SPECTACLE OF GABF

**B**ESIDES OKTOBERFEST and the harvest, the other huge and important thing that happens every fall is the Great American Beer Festival. From humble beginnings in 1982, it has grown into a true behemoth, showcasing hundreds of breweries and thousands of beers over its three days.

Sprawling over the better part of Denver's convention center, GABF is an earthly paradise for beer lovers. A single admission price gets you a glass and unlimited 1-ounce samples of whatever beers you want to try. It's a pilgrimage for every true beer lover, but the sheer size and scope of it can be a little intimidating.

Beyond the basics for any beer festival, such as pacing yourself, remembering to eat, and trying to have some kind of a plan, here are a few GABF-specific tips to help you get the most from your experience.

- **Book early.** Like most beer festivals, this one sells out quickly.

- **The Farm to Table Pavilion** in the back offers a relaxed, uncrowded atmosphere, fine food, and plenty of great beers, well worth the additional cost.

- **Head straight** for the American Cheese Society's booth near the center of the hall. Great beers, great cheese, and company representatives to help explain the essentials for you.

- **Stop by the bookstore** and hobnob with your favorite beer authors scheduled for signings. Signed books make great gifts!

- **Thursday night and Saturday afternoon** (American Homebrewers Association members only) are the best sessions, with many brewers manning their booths. Skip Saturday night if you can; it's the rowdiest of the week.

- **Don't forget** the many activities in the hall, such as beer and food demonstrations and "You Be the Judge," an introduction to how the competition is conducted.

- **Not all the great breweries have huge lines.** Check out lists of past winners for some fabulous breweries that not everyone will know about.

- **Spend some time at the Pro-Am booth.** These are beers created by homebrewers and brewed by commercial breweries and are often of fantastic quality.

- **Stop by the Brewers Association booth** and give founder and visionary Charlie Papazian a big thanks for all he's done for the sake of good beer over the years. Likewise for fest director Nancy Johnson or any of the rest of the dedicated staff.

- **Skip the pretzel necklace.** You look like a total dork. A string of tasty sausages would be cool, though.

- **There's plenty to do outside the festival:** bus tours, tastings, beer dinners, and more. Colorado's Front Range has a world-class brewing scene, and breweries or brewpubs are perfect for daytime or after-fest excursions.

# THE RISE OF THE PUMPKIN BEERS

**T**HE NORTH AMERICAN colonies were an inhospitable place for beer. Malt was in short supply, as New England and the southern colonies were poorly suited to barley cultivation. Hops were rarely grown in the colonies, and they did not often arrive in good condition when imported. It's no wonder that most people drank spirits or cider. Nevertheless, there was a demand for beer as a cheap and safe source of hydration and calories. Some beers, as George Washington's famous handwritten recipe shows, used molasses or other sugar as a source of fermentables. Almost every conceivable ingredient was used to create alcohol and add flavor to these rustic beers. Pumpkin, often preserved by drying, was one of them. With the industrialization of the country and the arrival of the Germans, with their well-developed brewing culture and technology, rustic beers with ingredients like pumpkin were forgotten.

Fast-forward 200 years or so. In 1982, a young entrepreneur named Bill Owens opened Buffalo Bill's Brewpub in Hayward, California; by 1986, he hit upon the idea of making a pumpkin beer. While the pilot batches were brewed with actual pumpkin, Owens found that the classic pie spices of cinnamon, nutmeg, allspice, and others were key to creating a pumpkin beer flavor, so the actual pumpkin was dropped from his production batches. Success grew beyond the confines of his pub and spawned a whole tradition of releasing pumpkin beers in the early fall.

A typical pumpkin beer will be a deep orange-ish amber in color, moderate in gravity and alcohol, and only lightly hopped. While most do contain some pumpkin, the vegetable's delicate flavor is almost always masked by the added pie spices. In fact, the overbearing nature of the spices is a frequent subject of debate on the online beer forums, because it can be problematic from a drinkability standpoint. Most feel a light touch makes the best beers. At their best, pumpkin beers should have a complex, delicate spiciness, a creamy texture, rich caramelly notes, and, yes, even a hint of the pumpkin itself.

## Crazy for Pumpkin Beers?

Try the Great Pumpkin Beer Festival in Seattle, at Elysian Brewing Company. Elysian's Dick Cantwell has long been a pioneer of exotically flavored beers and pours a lot of his personal passion into this fascinating little beer festival, which takes place in early October. With more than 60 pumpkin-oriented beers on tap over three days, there are plenty of uniquely squashy beers to choose from: pumpkin rye, sour pumpkin ale, barrel-aged pumpkin porter, sour cranberry pumpkin ale, pumpkin gruit, pumpkin stout, imperial pumpkin ale, ginger pumpkin pils, coffee pumpkin ale, and pumpkin dunkel weizenbock. Don't miss the tapping of the giant pumpkin filled with beer!

# SCARIEST BEERS FOR
# HALLOWEEN

### Rogue Dead Guy Ale

It's a year-round beer that has nothing in particular to do with fall, but you gotta love that name this time of year. And when the beer comes in an enameled bottle with a glow-in-the-dark skeleton on it, we'll find a way to make the beer work this time of year. Malty, but not too sweet, and nicely balanced by Rogue's trademark hoppiness. 6.5% ABV.

### 5 Rabbit Vide y Muerte

This is a beer I cooked up for the Chicago-area brewery in which I am a partner. We start with an Oktoberfest-type wort with plenty of Vienna malt, and a big, thick, gooey dollop of dulce de leche. The beer also has tiny amounts of Mexican cinnamon, allspice, and tarragon. As a result, the beer tastes quite a bit like graham crackers. 6.3% ABV.

### Great Lakes Nosferatu

Named for an early expressionist vampire film, this is a big blood-red ale with a heaping helping of the burnt raisin and caramel malt flavor that is the style's signature flavor, with a splash of hops for balance and a complex citrus-and-resin aroma. 8% ABV.

### AleSmith Evil Dead Red

A deeply colored red ale in the modern manner, which is to say plenty of burnt sugar flavors that are more than balanced by characterful American hops. 6.66% (get it?) ABV.

### Avery Mephistopheles

This is a huge imperial stout from one of the well-established breweries in Boulder, Colorado. Big, brooding, and definitely dangerous at 18% ABV.

### Capital Autumnal Fire

One of my seasonal favorites from this lager-oriented Wisconsin brewery. It's a simple beer, just a classic Oktoberfest recipe, but brewed at bock strength, it's extra delish. 7.8% ABV.

ROUNDUP OF **November** EVENTS

# LEARN TO HOMEBREW Day

Organized by the American Homebrewers Association; local clubs open their doors for beginners to receive some expert advice on the best way to start brewing. Usually the first Saturday in November.

## Festival of BARREL-AGED BEER
### Chicago, Illinois

It's not the biggest fest around, but you'd be hard-pressed to find a bigger batch of interesting and esoteric beers anywhere on the planet. This single-day event in Chicago draws forward-thinking brewers from all over the United States, with a heavier concentration from the Chicago area and the upper Midwest. FOBAB features both conventional barrel-aged beers and sour/wild creations that have spent time in the barrel. Presented by the Illinois Craft Brewers Guild; usually the second Saturday in November.

## Beer Weeks

- **Portland Beer Week (Oregon)**

- **Wilmington Beer Week (Delaware)**

- **NTX Beer Week (Texas)**

- **Dallas Beer Week (Texas)**

- **Houston Beer Week (Texas)**

- **Western Australia Beer Week**

## SAN DIEGO BEER WEEK

When is it *not* craft beer week in San Diego? Seriously, though, the week kicks off the first couple of days early in the month with the San Diego Brewers Guild Festival.

## TASMANIAN INTERNATIONAL
### Beerfest

Held in Hobart on the island of Tasmania, this is Australia's biggest beer festival, featuring dozens of breweries and cider companies, with a sprinkling of spirits thrown in. Friday and Saturday in mid-November.

## Other Fests

Arkansas Times Craft Beer Festival, North Little Rock, Arkansas · International Great Beer Expo, Elmont (Long Island), New York · Texas Brewvolution, kicking off North Texas Beer Week, Dallas, Texas · Caribbean Rum and Beer Festival, Grand Anse, St. George's, Granada · Mondial de la Bière, Rio de Janeiro, Brazil · Thai Beer Festival, Bangkok, Thailand · Mexicali Beer Fest, Mexico · Bierfest, Capetown, South Africa

# TURKEY TIME!

**THANKSGIVING** is fall's last blast. After that we are propelled into the holiday cyclone, and before you know it the year is over. Founded to celebrate a successful harvest, Thanksgiving has turned into a time for either celebrating — or enduring — the family, depending on your perspective. Either way, a little alcohol is a helpful thing.

The question is, what beer pairs with a feast? While the main dish of roast turkey is simple enough to match, the cacophony of classic sides, such as herbed stuffing, creamy gravy, marshmallow-y sweet potatoes, and tangy cranberry sauce, complicates matters. And since it's a family affair, it's not just you and your geeked-out pals trading IPA stories. Grandpa wants his Bud; Aunt Shirley likes her white

Zin a little too much; Uncle Stu is strictly about a perfect Manhattan; and your loser cousin Todd actually thinks Heineken is cool. Of course, some of these are lost causes, but what can you pop open that most of the family will actually enjoy?

Despite the heavy doses of gravy and butterfat, much of this food is actually fairly delicate on the palate. This means it's a good idea to stay away from anything too hoppy or roasty — which is also important when dealing with casual beer enjoyers. The simplest choice would be to go with the smooth, clean flavors of lagers. A nice maibock or blond doppelbock would serve nicely, and even a hearty interpretation of an Oktoberfest could work just fine. The next step up in sophistication would be to jump over the Rhine to Belgium. These beers were made to go with delicately flavored, slightly rich foods. They're delicate enough to not interfere with the subtle flavors of a simple dish like mashed potatoes, but they have

**A NICE MAIBOCK** or blond doppelbock complements the Thanksgiving feast.

enough alcohol and carbonation to deal with cream gravy. For the main event, I'm thinking along the lines of a tripel: blond, fizzy, crisp, just a bit complex in the nose, with the added benefit of being every bit as elegant and celebratory as Champagne. If you've got a beer-savvy crowd to please, you could even go with a Flemish sour red or brown ale like Duchesse de Bourgogne or Liefmans Goudenband. With a touch of acidity and a rich, round, malty character, both of these function as a Pinot Noir might, contrasting with the meat and potatoes on the plate and acting as a foil to the sweetness of the candied yams and cranberries. If you're going all-out and have a group that would appreciate it, Allagash Curieux, a bourbon barrel–aged tripel, is stunning in this situation, and not half bad with pecan pie, either.

For dessert, it's a good idea to ramp up the beers considerably. Sweet and fat are big tastes in the mouth and can soak up a lot of malt, roastiness, hops, and/or alcohol in the beer. For pumpkin pie, I find a rich American-style brown ale or even a Baltic porter to be a nice counterpoint. If you're having pecan pie, a Belgian strong dark typically offers complex, caramelly flavors and enough alcohol and carbonation to slice through the richness. Or, with the amount of teeth-ringing sweetness in that dish, an imperial red ale or barleywine can be a fine companion. And just remember, in case Mom burns the pie, those kinds of beers aren't bad *for* dessert, either.

CHAPTER SIX

Winter

6

# Winter will be your season of discontent

only if you can't stand strong beers. Cold temperatures really call out for big flavors and a certain amount of alcohol. It's no wonder that the English term for them is *winter warmers*. These days, there is no shortage of beers that suit that term. It's great to see the excitement around seasonal beers in general, and especially a bit of frenzy around the special releases for the holidays.

While a Midwestern winter is normally nothing to get too excited about, I sometimes find that I am actually looking forward to a little chill in the air. As I stockpile strong, cellar-worthy beers through the year, they sit on the shelf until the appropriate season comes along, as they're kind of a waste in warmer months, I think. So, come on snow, sleet, ice. Old Man Winter, do your worst. I've got beer to drink.

# WASSAIL AND HOLIDAY BEERS

**PEOPLE HAVE BEEN** making a fuss over Christmas since *way* before it was Christmas. The winter solstice that occurs at that time of the year is a big deal. Without some celebration, we would all be

As these antique Scandinavian labels show, there is a long and charming tradition of special holiday beers in the chilly North.

Flip is a hot beverage made with ale, eggs, and other flavorings caramelized with a red-hot poker, or "loggerhead."

plunged into an interminable cold, dark future — a dread we northerners know all too well around the end of February. A little strong beer is a great way to take the chill off and celebrate the renewal of spring even though it's down the road a ways.

While our predecessors undoubtedly drank less small beer and more full-strength beer in the winter, there is not a lot of evidence for winter-specific and holiday beers until around the second half of the twentieth century. Our ever-changing, variety-mad craft beer marketplace is a very recent thing in the long history of beer. Most people had very limited choices.

People in earlier times did like to spice up their drinking with special compounded beverages based on beer, with spices, sugar, wine, or spirits and enhancers such as cream or eggs. To help warm everyone's cockles, many of them were heated, sometimes in a copper "ale boot," a shoe-shaped vessel whose toe could

The church is near, but the road is icy;
THE PUB IS FAR, BUT
WE WILL WALK CAREFULLY.
– Russian proverb

be pushed into the coals at the edge of the hearth, gently warming the ale.

The beverage most associated with the winter solstice and Christmas is wassail. It serves as inspiration for many modern American spiced holiday ales despite being cider — rather than beer — based. Nevertheless, wassail's cinnamon, cloves, nutmeg, and ginger, added to a strongish dark ale, is a pretty typical recipe for a holiday ale. Anchor's Our Special Ale was the original in this vein, created in the mid-1980s. Spiced winter ales can be delightful, but a brewer needs to use a light touch with the spicing to prevent them from being overbearing and tiresome.

Probably because of the propensity of mud-colored spiced beers to overwhelm the palate, brewers have been moving toward alternatives for some time. Many are simply strong, darkish brews loosely in the English strong ale tradition. Pyramid's Snow Cap was an early stalwart.

Sierra Nevada's Celebration Ale takes a distinctly American tack. At 6.8% ABV, it's a modestly strong take on the company's house style, deep amber, packed with raisiny caramel malts and dripping with American C-hops: Cascade, Centennial, and Chinook varieties, fresh from the fall harvest.

## WARM BEER AND SPICES

**Crambambull**

Here are a few quick recipes for these venerable old beverages, sure to get your juices flowing.

**Crambambull** This is the name for an eggnog made with ale. The recipe calls for mixing up a classic eggnog base, then blending it with beer and perhaps a dash of rum, bourbon, or brandy at serving time.

Eggnog base: Separate 4 eggs, then whisk the yolks with ⅓ cup muscovado or turbinado sugar until the sugar dissolves. Add 2 cups whole milk, 1 cup heavy cream (whipped if you like an extra-fluffy texture), and ½ teaspoon freshly grated nutmeg — more or less to taste — and perhaps a tiny pinch of cinnamon, if you like. Then whip the egg whites to soft peaks, add 1 teaspoon regular granulated sugar, and continue whipping to stiff peak stage. Then fold into the rest of the mixture and chill.

To serve: Start with 4 ounces of your favorite holiday beer, ½ ounce of your choice of booze, and then top with 6 ounces of the nog base and enjoy.

**Flip** This an ancient hot beverage that was a cherished tradition a couple of centuries ago. After simmering the ingredients together for a short time, a red-hot poker called a loggerhead is jabbed into the mix, where it heats and caramelizes the beverage. Big holiday fun as long as you keep the kids — and everything else — away from the red-hot poker.

Combine 4 cups strong ale, 2 ounces aged rum, ¼ cup muscovado or turbinado sugar, ¼ teaspoon cinnamon, 2 whole cloves (or a pinch of ground), and a strip of lemon zest in a saucepan. Simmer, but don't boil, then turn off the heat and remove the cloves and lemon peel. Beat 4 whole eggs, and then gradually add some of the warm ale mixture to the eggs, stirring constantly. Finally, add the beaten egg mixture to the rest of the ale and beat passionately until it foams a little. To be authentic, heat up a well-washed iron bar or fireplace poker to a cherry-red color, then carefully (and maybe with eye protection) plunge it into the drink, where it will bubble and fume spectacularly. You could instead just heat it a bit more on the stovetop.

The final step is a little more frothing. Flip was also known as "Yard of Flannel," because it was frothed up by pouring from cup to cup, and accomplished mixers could do this in a pretty show-offy way, making a long tan stream from glass to glass. You can simply whip out the whisk or electric mixer and foam away. Flip was traditionally served in a large tapered glass tumbler, which was passed from person to person.

**Bishop** Bake an orange studded with 4 whole cloves until soft, about 30 minutes at 250°F (121°C). Quarter the orange, remove the seeds, and put the slices in a saucepan with 2 cups strong ale and 1 tablespoon raw sugar, and heat not quite to boiling. Remove from the heat and allow the drink to cool to a drinkable temperature. Serve in mugs; place a small pat of butter on top if you'd like to gild the lily.

Flip

Bishop

# ROUNDUP OF December EVENTS

**With the mad hubbub of the holidays and the chilly temperatures in many places, there aren't all that many major beer events in December. But you should check your local listings, as there are lots of small events, ugly-sweater parties, charity fundraisers, and other means of lifting your holiday spirits.**

## KERSTBIER
### Fest

(Christmas Beer Festival) A very special fest in Essen, near Antwerp, Belgium, focuses exclusively on the very characterful — and strong — Belgian Christmas beers. Six nights, five days midmonth.

## PORTLAND HOLIDAY
### Beer Festival

Held in heated tents under an immense decorated Christmas tree in downtown Portland, Oregon, this five-day fest features winter-themed craft beers of all stripes, "from Belgians to barleywines to stouts to sours," many of them special editions that aren't available anywhere else. Early December.

# ENGLISH WINTER WARMERS AND MORE

**F**OR DECADES, English brewers have been making winter warmers that offer a bit more alcohol than standard bitter and pale ales, typically ranging from 5 to 8% ABV or occasionally higher, and usually with a burnished mahogany color, a dense creamy foam, and a balance hewing close to the brewery's house character. With a really good one, your attention bounces from nutty sweetish malt to hops to toast and round and round, chasing its own tail in the most captivating way. Served on cask, a beer like this can be a feast for the senses.

The term *warmer* is commonly applied to rich and typically dark winter seasonal brews, although not all brewers use this term for the style. *Strong ale* is a common descriptor in the UK, but in the United States, the Tax and Trade Bureau (TTB) does not allow terms of strength on beer labels, so a variety of other terms are used. Some English terms are regional — for example, *stingo* in Yorkshire.

Two for your consideration: Fuller's Old Winter Ale (4.8% ABV), sort of a dark and malty mild in their house style, with a minimal hop presence; and Young's Winter Warmer (5.0% ABV), brewed from Maris Otter malt seasoned with Fuggle and Golding hops, lightened up with the brewery's "unique cane sugar mix."

Part of the same family of strong British beers, *old ale* is a sometimes a carelessly applied term meaning that some or all of the beer has undergone extensive aging in oak. The wood's porosity makes it a haven for a number of wild microbes, most notably *Brettanomyces*, which can add aromas reminiscent of a barnyard or pineapple candy. Historically the aged character was referred to as "stale." *Stale* wasn't a negative and didn't mean spoiled or sour, as the old books of the period always have a chapter dedicated to remedies for that sorry condition.

# A ZWARTE PIET CHRISTMAS

**I**N AMERICA, we have the obese, jolly, cookie- and Coke-loving Santa, but not all children have such an affable benefactor at Christmastime. In the Alps and adjacent parts of Europe, a sort of anti-Santa called Krampus seeks out wicked children, removing them to his lair for what can only be assumed to be reprogramming. Saint Nicholas has a malevolent companion in Belgium: Zwarte Piet, or "Black Pete," a colorfully dressed reformed devil (or freed Moorish slave — whichever story you prefer), face stained black from chimney entrances. He leaves gifts in the children's shoes, and fortunately, there might just be room in there for a special bottle of beer. Belgians celebrate December 6 and the eve before to honor him and his benefactor, Sinterklaas, their name for St. Nicholas.

Belgian brewers love to celebrate the holidays with special versions of their beers. They are usually just amped-up versions of already strong beers, sometimes a little darker in color. Be careful. Normal Belgian beers are alarmingly drinkable, and these extra-strong cuvées are doubly dangerous. Here are a few Christmas specialties that might taste great for a pre-holiday soirée. Don't forget to leave your shoes out.

# 12 BEERS OF CHRISTMAS

### Anchor Christmas Ale
Like so many things emanating from Anchor, this beer, launched in 1975, revived the tradition of special holiday beers in the United States, inspiring many others. At first it was unseasoned, but the brewery soon switched to an assertively spiced recipe that varied widely from year to year. Anchor's tradition is to be absolutely secretive about the recipe. While not meant to age, these beers are fun to taste as a mini vertical. 5.5% ABV.

### Three Floyds Alpha Klaus
In keeping with the Floyd's house style, this is an unspiced classic American porter, meaning it has a buttload of West Coast hops, building citrus and plywood notes on top of a very rich chocolaty porter lightened up a little by the use of Mexican unrefined sugar. Long, bittersweet cocoa finish. 6.0% ABV.

### Samuel Smith's Winter Welcome
One of the first English winter warmers available in the United States, this widely available amber-brown beer is still a standard. With a rich, lightly creamy mouthfeel with hints of nuts and dried fruits, it is an unspiced beer in the classic tradition. 6.0% ABV.

### Birrificio Del Ducato Krampus
A wildly delicious *Brettanomyces*-inflected strongish spiced golden ale from a stellar brewery in northern Italy, it has a barnyard nose with clove and gumdrop overtones. It's named for Santa's avenging evil twin, appropriately enough, since this pale, dry, and very wild creation is everything most Christmas beers are not. 7.0% ABV.

### Breckenridge Christmas Ale
A classic American craft take on a winter warmer, with caramel and chocolate flavors balanced by loads of rich, fruity notes and some slightly citrus-peel hops. Liquid fruitcake! 7.4% ABV.

### Anderson Valley Winter Solstice
This long-running craft operation in the stunningly beautiful valley northeast of the Sonoma wine region has long been famous for its generously hopped beers. 7.9% ABV.

**Thirsty Dog 12 Dogs of Christmas** This Akron, Ohio–based brewery is a bit of a hidden treasure — unless you live in northern Ohio, of course. This dark ruby brew has a classic honeyed spice-cake nose, rich toffee and toast on the palate, and a long, fruity, bittersweet finish. 8.3% ABV.

**Brasserie de la Senne Equinox/Zwarte Piet** A rich, dark Belgian ale with raisiny flavors and a slightly chocolaty finish from brewer Yvan DeBaets, who is also a beer historian and author. 8% ABV.

example, "two turtle doves" translated to a chocolate pecan (a.k.a. Turtles candy) beer. Alcohol varies between 10 and 12% ABV.

**Troeg's Mad Elf** This cherry-infused beer was rated number one in Joe Sixpack's (Don Russell) book *Christmas Beers*, and this eastern Pennsylvania beer is definitely a contender. With sweet and sour cherries, lightened a bit with some local honey, it's a gloriously festive, ruby-red mouthful that's *way* too easy to drink. 11% ABV.

**Affligem Noël** Luscious, softly chocolaty beer in the Belgian strong dark pantheon. Plenty of dark dried fruit notes: cherries, plums, and more. A little hops for balance plus brewer's caramel sugar to give it a really deadly drinkability — in a good way, of course. 9.0% ABV.

**The Bruery "12 Days of Christmas" Series** Every year, the beer in this series (begun in 2008) varies widely and reflects, as much as possible, the familiar song lyrics. For

**Schmaltz Brewing Jewbelation Ale** In keeping with the importance of symbolic numbers in the Hebraic tradition, each year's edition uses the same number of malts and hops as the anniversary year, and the alcohol content keeps pace as well. After a decade and a half, the beer is pretty big and complex, and it's almost easier to say what's *not* in it. Rich, deep, brooding, and dark, it's sugar-plums in a glass. At this point in the series, it's 15% ABV and higher.

# ROUNDUP OF January EVENTS

## ALASKAN BEER AND BARLEYWINE Festival

Alaska in January? Sure, why not. This long-running fest in Anchorage gives you plenty of reasons to stay indoors and enjoy the great beers and extra-cozy Alaskan camaraderie. A great festival with lots of side events, a mini homebrewing conference, and more, it's also a fundraiser for the American Diabetes Association. Midmonth; coincides with Alaska Beer Week, with plenty of fun events to keep you warm.

## BIG BEERS, BELGIANS & BARLEY-WINES Festival

This food-centric event in the luxury ski resort of Vail, Colorado, draws rave reviews from brewers and attendees alike. Not just a festival, but lots of tasting events, dinners, educational seminars, and more. Ski off the night's beers on the slopes in the morning before the fun begins. Second week.

## Other Fests

Beer Dabbler
Winter Carnival,
St. Paul, Minnesota

## Beer Weeks

• **Alaska Beer Week**

• **Kalamazoo Beer Week (Michigan)**

• **South Florida Beer Week**

# A SHORT HISTORY OF BARLEYWINE

**A**S THE GALES SWIRL and the snow builds up, there is nothing so comforting as a snifter of really strong ale to sip by the fireplace. There are plenty of choices here, but the deepest, darkest days of winter call out for the king of all strong beers: barleywine.

While most of us enthusiasts in the United States think of it as a defined style, barleywine has never really been much more than a poetic term for any strong beer. In England, that generally meant a strong "October" beer, most famously brewed on country estates in private brewhouses. Luminously amber, loaded with hops and a complex vinous aroma due to extended aging in oak casks, these prized beers were the precursors to modern IPAs. A special brewing technique called double mashing allowed alcohol strength in some special versions to climb well over 10% ABV, definitely into wine territory.

At their best, such beers coax massive complexity out of just a few high-quality ingredients such as the heirloom Marris Otter malt and East Kent Golding hops, making them the conceptual equivalent of something like a Grand Cru Burgundy, dependent on very special ingredients and local terroir.

*Barleywine* was first used as a descriptor in marketing by Bass Brewery, applying the term to their massive (10% ABV) Number 1 sometime prior to 1900. Other English brewers applied it occasionally to their strong, but not necessarily mind-numbing, beers. Sometimes the term can be found on beers around 6% ABV. It's actually fairly challenging to find a British beer that's labeled as a barleywine, although many strong beers exist.

At any rate, the term caught the imagination of American craft brewers. Anchor, in San Francisco, was the first to release one — by a mile — launching their Old Foghorn as early as 1975. Since then, most U.S. barleywines have followed the Foghorn model: strong, rich, deeply amber, and loaded with hops, but numerous variations exist. The End. I told you it was short.

Barleywines are perfect winter beers because of their sippably strong nature. There are certainly many more examples out there, especially from American breweries, but here are a handful of classics:

### J. W. Lee's Harvest Ale

A glorious beer strictly in the manner of the grand old October beers, pure and simple. Nothing but the rare heirloom malt Maris Otter, plus East Kent Goldings hops, but there's a world of complexity in every bottle. Ages very gracefully.

### Thomas Hardy's Ale

Created by Eldridge Pope in 1968, this classic was inspired by a description of a fine aged Dorchester beer in one of Hardy's novels, *The Trumpet Major*. When the Eldridge Pope brewery closed in 1999, it went out of production, a symptom of the woes surrounding Britain's heritage breweries. However, it wasn't that long ago that Hardy's was universally hailed as the king of all cult beers. Deep in color, complex, and very long-lived, it seems to be back on the market again. Let's hope that this time it will stick around long enough to assemble a proper vertical tasting in future years.

### Anchor Old Foghorn

Still regarded as the model of the style, Foghorn has a deep reddish amber color and a complex vinous aroma from several months aging at the brewery, with plenty of burnt sugar notes and a refined hop character.

### Bigfoot Barleywine

This is a brash American attack on the style from Sierra Nevada. Introduced in 1983, it features a toasted toffee malt character, slathered with fresh, citrus-floral American hops. The brewery philosophy is to use whole hops rather than pelletized; they claim cleaner, softer flavors are the result. This beer certainly delivers. While founder Ken Grossman and his crew generally prefer Bigfoot as fresh and in-your-face as possible, they admit the beer ages pleasantly, drying out, picking up sherrylike aged character and undergoing a softening of the hop bite.

# AGED BEER AND VERTICAL TASTINGS

**A**N INFALLIBLE way to amuse one's friends in the depths of winter is to present a vertical tasting. This refers not to the position of the tasters, but rather to a flight of beers presented in a succession of years released, going vertically back in time. This requires the type of big beers so well suited to the winter season.

Not every beer will gracefully bear aging, but some hold up remarkably well. I once tasted a beer from 1938, which was 66 years old at the time. It was a fascinating ghost, but a younger beer in the same flight had borne its 46 years very gracefully. The old English books are full of references to "nut brown" and October beers aged for a decade or more that were still breathtakingly delicious. Even their standard versions were routinely aged for at least a year before the barrel was breached. An extra-strong beer called a double ale was brewed by a unique mashing method in which the same liquid was run through two successive mashes, effectively doubling up the malt — and therefore the alcohol. Such beers were sometimes called majority ales, as they were often brewed upon the birth of a son and not tapped until he was 21.

Aging your own beers requires a similarly long view, although great results can be had in much less time. First rule: Start with big beers. With the exception of lambics and some other sour beers that play by their own weird rules, it takes a lot of malt, hops, and alcohol to

Another major enemy of aging beer is light, so keep it dark. Those living in warmer climates will have to resort to some specialized storage; many of my California beer buddies rent wine lockers in the climate-controlled facilities that are everywhere in that oenophilic state. Refrigeration is not recommended, as it slows down the aging to a crawl.

In general, beer should not be aged on its side. The only exception would be cork-sealed beers destined for five years or more of aging. In that case, storing a beer on its side keeps the cork hydrated and the bottle sealed. Once stored, leave them be. If you are a person of weak will, store the beer at a non-drinking relative's house where you won't be tempted. Think like a squirrel: Stash away beers in safe places whenever you can, and try to forget about them for a while.

Over time, a number of changes occur. Hops become much more subdued, losing as much as half their aroma and bitterness in the course of a year or so. In time, yeasty fruitiness will fade, and the perception of maltiness will increase as competing flavors diminish. The body will thin out, and over time the head retention and possibly

withstand the ravages of time. The lower limit is about 8% ABV, and if you're thinking decades, over 10% ABV is a good place to start. Bottle-conditioned and other unfiltered beers age better, the yeast providing some oxygen-scavenging protection and adding layers of flavor, just as in a vintage Champagne. Beer ages better if it's alive.

In temperate climates, a cellar works fine as a resting place. Seasonal swings are fine if you can keep the cellar from becoming too warm in the summer. Around 70°F (21°C) or below is a good target. Obviously, preventing the beer from freezing in the winter is mandatory. What your sleeping beer really does not like is frequent temperature swings, as they tend to disrupt the protein structure critical for body and head retention. Do what you can to insulate your cellar to keep the temperature as constant as you can.

carbonation will be reduced, as caps are not an absolutely gas-tight seal. A certain pleasant oxidized flavor I think of as a bit leathery will build, along, perhaps, with some sherry- or port-like nuttiness. After a decade or so, some autolyzed, soy sauce flavors will emerge from the failing yeast, and the beer may lose all carbonation and a good deal of color as well.

It's a fascinating trip back through time, and you'll notice changes between every vintage. Even beers brewed from identical recipes and stored under the same conditions will age differently from each other. Minor year-to-year variations in the barley-growing conditions are magnified during storage, reminding us that beer is an agricultural product.

What to age? Barleywine, of course, plus any other strong ale, imperial stout, or imperial anything, really. Belgian strong dark ales and other strong specialties sometimes change in appealing ways.

Traditional lambics generally have a whole community of microflora in the bottle, so they will continue to evolve in the bottle, becoming more complex, drier, and acidic over time. Beers bottled with the wild yeast *Brettanomyces,* such as the famous Trappist beer Orval, will develop barnyard aromas and maybe a pineapple fruitiness as they age over the course of a few years. With the possible exception of eisbocks, don't bother with lagers, as they're generally aged to perfection before leaving the brewery and don't further develop after packaging.

Vertical tasting is a great group activity for obvious reasons, not the least of which is the challenge of drinking several bottles of strong beer in a single session. It is helpful to spread the cost around as well, since age-worthy beers are not cheap. A beer vertical tasting can be tremendously educational and a very special beer experience. Don't forget to take notes.

DRINK TODAY AND DROWN ALL SORROW; You shall perhaps not do it tomorrow; Best, while you have it, use your breath; There is no drinking after death. –John Fletcher

# ROUNDUP OF FEBRUARY EVENTS

## TORONADO BARLEYWINE Festival

This stalwart craft beer bar in San Francisco hosts one of the longest-running events dedicated to these strong and luscious ales. Festgoers crowd into the cozy bar to sample more than 50 draft barleywines. It's the one can't-miss event of San Francisco Beer Week. Near the end of the month.

## BAB BIERFESTIVAL

Hosted by the Brugse Autonome Bierproevers, the Bruges, Belgium, tasters' society, this fest features more than 70 Belgian brewers and a bewildering variety of delicious Belgian beers. Bruges is like a beer Disneyland anyway; this event turns it into a glorious paradise for a couple of days. The first weekend of February.

## The CAMRA NATIONAL Winter Ales Festival

**Manchester, United Kingdom (has also been celebrated in Glasgow and Burton-on-Trent). Third weekend.**

## PIANETTA BIRRA

Sort of like a beer festival, but really it's the all-Italy bar and nightclub trade show, as there are a ton of booths representing Italy's exciting new beer scene. Rimini (a beach town on the Adriatic), in February.

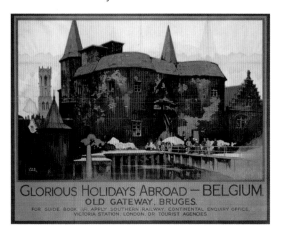

GLORIOUS HOLIDAYS ABROAD — BELGIUM.
OLD GATEWAY, BRUGES.

FOR GUIDE BOOK (1H) APPLY SOUTHERN RAILWAY CONTINENTAL ENQUIRY OFFICE, VICTORIA STATION, LONDON, OR TOURIST AGENCIES

**CELEBRATE:**

# INTERNATIONAL GRUIT DAY, FEBRUARY 1

A worldwide (well, U.S. mostly) celebration of this ancient unhopped beer.

## Beer Weeks

- **Cincinnati Beer Week (Ohio)**

- **San Francisco Beer Week (California)**

- **Omaha Beer Week (Nebraska)**

- **Arizona Beer Week**

- **New York Craft Beer Week**

- **Sacramento Beer Week (California)**

- **Portsmouth Beer Week (New Hampshire)**

- **Southwest Australia Craft Beer Week**

# Other Fests

Winterfest, Minnesota Craft Brewers Guild, St. Paul, Minnesota · **Buffalo Winter BrewFest, Buffalo, New York** · International Great Beer Expo New Jersey, Secaucus, New Jersey · **Rhode Island Brew Fest, Pawtucket, Rhode Island** · Winter Beer Carnival, Atlanta, Georgia · **Cincy Winter Beerfest, Cincinnati, Ohio** · Zwickelmania (Oregon Brewers Guild presents brewery open houses), in various locations across Oregon · **Philly Bierfest, German Society of Pennsylvania, Philadelphia, Pennsylvania** · Adelaide Schuetzenfest, Australia · **Elmar's Food & Beer Festival, Perth, Australia**

# SKIP THE CHAMPAGNE:
# BEERS TO RING IN THE NEW YEAR

**CHAMPAGNE** always seems like such a waste on New Year's Eve. Celebratory as it is, it's really much better as an aperitif, best served to wake up everyone's palate at the beginning of an evening, not to cap off a night of eating and drinking. A special beer might convey the correct jubilant mood, but do it in a way that cuts through the gastronomic clutter of a long session. Here are a few of my favorites.

**Méthode Champenoise Beers** If you want to preserve that classic bubbly experience, these might be the ticket. There are just a few of them, and they are crazy expensive, but beers such as Bosteels Deus (Belgium) and Eisenbahn Lust (Brazil) offer a beery interpretation of the sparkling wine experience: crisp, dry, elegant, ghostly pale, and highly effervescent. And hey, it's only once a year.

**Double IPA** Of course you gotta love hops, but there is no doubt that these beers will punch through anything the winter can offer. Brisk, bracing, intense, and above all bitter, these will start the year off for you with a bang. Firestone Walker's Double Jack is very elegant; Dogfish Head 90 Minute has a touch of sweetness.

**Flemish Sour Red and Brown Ales** With their complex, oak-tinged aromas, crisp acidity, and slight sweetness, these beers are every bit as elegant and celebratory as Champagne. Typically blended from fresh beer mixed with a smaller amount of oak-aged sour beer, they offer luminous ruby hues and luscious yet refreshing flavors. The sourness varies from super-tangy to just a hint; some offer vinegary notes as well. Reds and browns come from slightly different regions of Flanders. The reds are perhaps a little more sharp and wine-like, while the browns are a bit more beery and creamy and maybe a bit earthier as well, but it's all a big happy family. Delicious cherry-spiked versions are made with both types.

**Kriek Lambic** These Belgian classic wild/sour beers have cherries added. Classic production dictates that the cherries, pits and all, are added to the barrel and left there until the flesh melts away and the beer develops a nice cherry fruitiness with the almond/kirsch aroma of the pits. Many breweries cheat a little these days, and while those beers can be enjoyable, the classics have a lot more character. To my taste, the 3 Fonteinen Oude Schaarbeekse Kriek, with its traditional heirloom cherries, is the king of the heap. If you forget to open it on the Eve, you can always have it for brunch the next day. Yummy.

**Eisbock: The Monster Lager** If there's a lager beer made just for subzero weather, this is the one. Smooth, malty, even syrupy in texture, and high in alcohol, it drinks like a liquid dessert. The term *eisbock* refers to a process in which the beer is frozen and the ice crystals that form are filtered out, concentrating the alcohol and everything else that's left behind. Historically associated with the German city of Kulmback, it's a German specialty, typically in the amber-to-brown bock style, lightly hopped, and starting at about 10% ABV but sometimes far exceeding

that. The Scottish craft brewery Brew Dog pushed the style further in its battle with German brewery Scorschbräu for the title of world's strongest beer: starting with Tactical Nuclear Penguin (32% ABV), firing back with Sink the Bismark (41% ABV), and ending on a bombshell with the appropriately named End of History (55% ABV), bottled in an extremely limited edition of taxidermy-encased bottles using the corpses of weasels, squirrels, and assorted small mammals.

Most eisbocks are much less histrionic. Look for beers such as G'frorns from Reichelbräu and the deliciously cake-like Adventinus Weizeneisbock from Schneider Weisse. Outside the occasional keg of "accidental" eisbock from a brewpub or homebrewer, there are few of them packaged in the United States, as the government considers the freeze-concentrating process to be distilling and won't allow its use in brewing. "Ice" beers from mass-market brewers do have ice removed, but water is then added back to restore the original alcohol content, achieving little but a marketing boast.

# BEER, CHOCOLATE, AND VALENTINE'S DAY

**EBRUARY 14** is a sommelier's worst nightmare: crowds of wine amateurs, advancing like zombies out of their suburban lairs, moaning, "Chocolate . . . Champagne!" In addition to wrecking the chocolate, this pairing turns a lovely and sophisticated sparkling wine into a screechy mouthful of virtual pickle juice. Beer to the rescue.

Because the malts that go into beer are kilned in ways that allow it to resemble chocolate or its natural companions — nuts, caramel, and dried fruits — it's easy to find great matches for Cupid's special date night. The rule about matching food and beer intensity applies here, and since chocolate is a powerful flavor on the palate, we'll need some fairly intense beers to go with it.

The chocolate and beer ladder at right will give you a general idea of what kind of beer might go with what kind of chocolate, but this is just a starting point. There's nothing wrong with purely chocolate flavors, but a bounty of other flavors can link specific beers with a compatible dish.

Consider a Belgian dubbel with its deep dried fruit notes served with chocolate-covered raisins or some fancier dish with similar flavors. Or maybe an English-style barleywine with its deep layers of caramel and toffee with a chocolate-bottomed pecan pie or caramel nut tart.

Don't forget about white chocolate. It can open up to a range of delicately flavored beers such as Belgian tripels or strong amber ales that would be clobbered by dark chocolate. With this combination, it's possible to incorporate fruits such as passion fruit or peaches, as well as lighter caramel or cooked sugar notes — think white chocolate and passion fruit crème brûlée or coconut and white chocolate cream pie.

As you move up the intensity scale on the chocolate side, you need to do the same with the beers. While pure chocolate bars are the ultimate in intense chocolate sensation, I find that because they take time to melt in your mouth, the beer is gone

## THE CHOCOLATE & BEER LADDER

| INTENSITY | BEER TYPE + FOOD |
|---|---|
| 4 | Belgian Tripel + White Chocolate Cheesecake |
| 5 | Oatmeal Stout + Peanut Butter Cups |
| 6 | Baltic Porter + Chocolate Brownies |
| 7 | Belgian Strong Dark Ale + Milk Chocolate |
| 8 | Imperial Red Ale + Flourless Chocolate Cake |
| 9 | Bourbon-Barrel Stout + Dark Chocolate Malted Milk Balls |
| 10 | Imperial Stout + Chocolate Truffles |

by then, whereas the lower melting point of chocolate truffles actually delivers a more intense chocolate blast on the palate. Of course, with truffles it's easy to incorporate all manner of twisted additional flavors, from ground chile to curry powder to chanterelles and beyond.

If you're an old married couple for whom Valentine's Day no longer crackles with electricity as it once did, a couple of big glasses of a rich, creamy porter and a plate of homemade chocolate chip cookies is a great relationship builder in the most comfortable way.

**Customize your truffles. Take any basic truffle recipe and roll in crushed malts such as crystal, brown, or black, or in very finely sieved powdered hops pellets.**

# A FEW
# NOT-SO-OBVIOUS
# WINTER BEERS

### Tropical Export Stout

It's amazing that a beer can be equally at ease whether you're frolicking on the beach in Jamaica or huddled by the fireplace, trapped by the blizzard raging outside. The style is essentially a goosed-up Irish stout, dry and espresso-like, with a bit of sweetness and a long, bitter espresso finish. Guinness Foreign Extra, first brewed in 1801, is the original, but Jamaica's Dragon Stout from Desnoes & Geddes has entrenched itself in the Caribbean over the past century. In Asia, Lion Stout occupies a similar role.

### Belgian Strong Golden Ale

Clean and hushed as a fresh snowfall, these deceptively strong blond beers can put Jack Frost in his place as convincingly as anything dark and heavy. Pure pilsner malt lends a clean, bright, bready flavor that's balanced by modest hopping, made more drinkable by the addition of sugar, and elegantly aromatized by a fruity Belgian yeast. The widely available Duvel is the gold standard, but there are bunches of them on the market these days. The closely related abbey tripel style may offer a little more honeyed depth.

and indulgently rich. Rogue's Hazelnut Brown Nectar is the widely available standard-bearer. Look for Perennial's Black Walnut Dunkel and Lazy Magnolia's Southern Pecan, and for a hit of the exotic, try Cervejaria Colorado's Berthô, a Brazil nut brown ale from Brazil.

**Scotch Ale** These strong, sweet, and super-malty beers seemed to have originated with similar beers first made famous in Burton-on-Trent, England. Whatever the history, they are as pure and malty as beer gets, with the barest minimum of hops way in the background for balance. Try one with sticky toffee pudding, the national dessert of Scotland.

**Strong Witbiers and White IPAs** These two closely related styles are recent inventions of the U.S. craft beer scene. Based on classic witbier recipes with wheat-and-oats creaminess, these both ramp up the gravity and alcohol. White IPAs take the next logical step and toss in a load of hops as well.

**Dark Mild Ale** While great examples are still elusive, these roasty yet light-bodied beers are getting better as well as easier to come by. They are aromatically malty and dry on the palate for superb drinkability, and I guess you could call them excellent snow-shoveling beers.

**Nut Beers** Maybe it's just because my dad always had his bowl of nuts at his side, industriously cracking and picking the meats out, that I associate them with the winter holidays. Most nut beers suit the season, being strong, sweet,

## A FEW WINTER BEER COCKTAILS

**Polish Coffee** Baltic porter (the stronger the better), enlivened with coffee liqueur such as Kahlúa, topped with whipped cream. Serve cold, in small glasses.

**Head-Bobber** Two parts Belgian amber such as Kwak, Barbär, or Atomium, one part hard cider, plus a splash of bauern obstler (unaged apple-pear brandy) or German brandy. Garnish with a cinnamon stick and/or cubed apple pieces on a skewer. Serve cold or warm.

**Hop Toddy** Double IPA with a dab of bourbon, a couple of teaspoons of honey, and a squeeze of lemon, plus half a dozen barely crushed juniper berries. Gently warm, and serve with a garnish of dried apricot.

# WILL IT EVER BE SPRING?

**T**HE TREES have budded out. A few wretched songbirds have migrated a little too early; the snow is at its blackest and sloppiest. It does seem about this time that winter is endless. But the signs of spring are there. Eventually, things will improve.

What to drink? To continue with those dark, fruitcakey winter beers at this moment seems like an admission of defeat. Something more optimistic is called for.

**Alaskan Winter Ale** Okay, the name is wintery, but the flavor is anything but. Inspired by research into Alaska's earliest brewing days and local tradition, founder Geoff Larson became intrigued by spruce tips, a nutrient-rich food resource long utilized by native peoples and occasionally incorporated into beer in pioneer days. Instead of the piney flavors expected, spruce tips add a deep dried fruit aroma with a slight spice. Plucked from the budding trees, this beer is quite literally the taste of spring.

**Capital Blonde Doppelbock** This well-established brewery near Madison, Wisconsin, focuses on lagers, with its most stellar products being fine seasonal bocks. This is among the strongest. Purely malty balanced with a light touch of hops, all wrapped up in the pure, clean flavors of a lager.

**Ayinger Weizenbock** While most in this style are a deep amber color and have a decided cake-like aroma, this one is a surprising blond color with a mellow, slightly caramelized ripe banana aroma and just a hint of spice. At 7.1% ABV, it's sturdy enough, but not overwhelming. Drink it outside, even if you have to wear a hat.

# ROUNDUP OF March EVENTS

## GREAT ARIZONA BEER Festival
**A charity benefit event in the typical festival mode, This features local as well as international beers. Tempe, Arizona; first weekend of the month.**

## Day of the LIVING ALES

A real ale festival organized by the Chicago Beer Society, the oldest beer appreciation society in the United States. The attraction is a wide range of American craft beers of all styles served on cask, most of which are unavailable in real ale form at any other time or place. Two sessions; typically the first Saturday in March.

## STARKBIER Madness!

Famous for its vast Oktoberfest, Munich hosts a lesser known and much more intimate beer festival in early spring: Starkbierfest. *Stark* simply means "strong" in German, so we're talking about bock beers here, strong members of the lager family. Many Münchners consider *Starkbierzeit* ("strong beer time") to be a fifth season, meant for cutting loose a little as spring approaches.

Events take place at breweries and beer halls all around Munich during the first two weeks of March, but the epicenter is the Paulaner Nockherberg Brewery, on the south side of town. With room for 2,500 revelers in its fest hall, there's plenty of fun to be had, especially with 7.5% ABV Salvator being served in 1-liter stoneware mugs — hoo-boy! As with Oktoberfest, reservations for tables are recommended for larger groups.

### CELEBRATE:
## ST. PATRICK'S DAY, MARCH 17

This Irish-American extravaganza has a reputation for being a real amateur's day, so caution is advised. A little pubbing around can be fun, but avoid the green beer and stick to the stout.

### CELEBRATE:
## MICHAEL JACKSON'S BIRTHDAY, MARCH 27

Writer Jackson was known as the "Bard of Beer," but this moniker barely hints at his various roles as enlightener, muse, poet, cheerleader, and steadfast friend of good beer wherever he found it. Hoist a toast with those you care about.

# Beer Weeks

- **Tampa Bay Beer Week (Florida)**

- **Traverse City Craft Beer Week (Michigan)**

- **Boston Beer Week (Massachusetts)**

- **Charlotte Craft Beer Week (North Carolina)**

- **Nashville Craft Beer Week (Tennessee)**

- **Colorado Craft Beer Week**

# Other Fests

Extreme Beer Fest (EBF) at the Seaport World Trade Center in Boston, Massachusetts (Third weekend) · New England Real Ale eXhibition (NERAX), North America's premier celebration of real ale, Boston, Massachusetts

# CHAPTER SEVEN

# AROUND
## the WORLD in
## 80 BEERS

7

# With your great thirst for beer experiences,

what if you won the lottery? If you had unlimited resources and no fear of jet lag, could you spend an entire year on the road, chasing down the great beer events like a surfer in search of the perfect wave? Let's assume for a moment that you could. This chapter is your itinerary.

The trip careens around the United States and back and forth to Europe a few times and hits South America and Australia by way of Hawaii. It's not a pretty path, zigging and zagging erratically, but that's the price to be paid for hitting every major beer event on the planet in one year. There are just a few R&R breaks here, but not too many. It's getting to be a pretty beery planet, and that means there is almost always some beer event worth traveling to going on somewhere.

This is all a fantasy, of course. No one's liver or attention span is really up to swallowing this many beers in one long continuous streak. But we all have dreams, and even the unattainable ones are a lot of fun to fantasize about. The listings here do point out some advantageous strings of events that will get you to several fabulous fests, one after the other in a logical way. If you can't give up two years of your life — one to travel this grueling itinerary and one to recover — hitting some shorter sections of the grand tour may be well within the realm of the possible.

Dates for these events do change from year to year, and they change names and even cease to exist. If you book a ticket to Bulgan Aimag, Mongolia, for the Fermented Mare's Milk Fest (mid-September) and don't check the dates first, don't blame me when you find that you just missed it and that it was really great.

Also, we're living in an age when there are more people wanting to attend these events than there are available spots, so tickets for many events sell out well in advance. Everything is done online these days, so get on it as soon as you can to get the best chance of snagging your pass.

As much fun as these festivals are, it's important to remember that beer travel is about much more. So plan some extra time on every trip to soak up the local life, pub culture, foods, history, and all of that. Many cities in Europe offer walking tours of historic neighborhoods that are actually pub crawls, and those are great whenever you can find them. Breweries offer tours, and there are many brewery museums in various parts of Europe. I love to visit art museums to look for pictures of people drinking beer and to drool all over the collections of antique glassware and ceramics, imagining what kind of delicious beer they must have held.

Traveling is always far better when you can connect with the locals. As beer enthusiasts and homebrewers, we are lucky, because we are all part of the secret society of beer. These days, it's easy enough to connect with beer fans anywhere online. Make plans in advance for a pub night out, or better yet, tell them you're bringing some rare and exciting beers or homebrew to sample, and you'll make some new friends who can help you understand their world. Also, check the online club calendars for regular meetings and events hosted by homebrew clubs or beer appreciation groups, and you may be lucky enough to get in on something really interesting. In many places, there are women-only tasting groups, so check those out if you qualify.

For the ultimate in beer-soaked travel, think about staying in breweries and pubs. It's easier than you might think, especially in Europe, so research that option wherever you're going. Germany actually has a Brauerei Gasthof (brewery guesthouse) association that publishes a guide to dozens of breweries that have rooms available for travelers.

ROUNDUP
**January**
EVENTS

*We'll start the world tour with a couple of big-ass beer festivals in some chilly but beautiful locations:*

### Big Beers, Belgians & Barleywines Festival, VAIL, COLORADO

Vail is among the most exclusive ski areas in the United States and as a result has a booming restaurant culture and lots of serious foodies hanging around. So, many of the events surrounding this festival have a heavy focus on food and draw brewers who share the passion for delicious food. There are dinners, seminars, workshops, and of course a grand tasting event featuring all that is strong and mighty in beer.

### Alaskan Beer and Barleywine Festival, ANCHORAGE, ALASKA

Alaska is a long way away in every sense, but when you get there you'll find the warmest possible kind of community. And during this week there are some seriously big beers there as well. This event is the capstone at the end of Alaska Beer Week, so you'll come early and take part in all that has to offer. Anchorage is a compact city with plenty of brewpubs and beer bars in a walkable downtown, with a few more just a short hop away. There are some really terrific beers, and it will great to be able to tell your friends you went to Alaska to drink barleywines in January and survived to tell the tale — assuming you do, of course. Third week.

### South Florida Beer Week, MIAMI, FLORIDA

Recover in the sun before heading off to Europe for a serious festathon. Florida and the rest of the southern United States have been a little late to the craft beer party, but things are changing fast thanks to progressive brewers like Tampa's Cigar City Brewing. This event takes place in the greater Miami area around the last week of the month. It's nice to be among the beautiful young things in southern Florida this time of year, and the food is great as well.

*Enjoy the respite and build up your energy reserves. You're going to need a stockpile before hopping on a plane to Europe for the next leg of the journey.*

## ROUNDUP FEBRUARY EVENTS

**BAB Bierfestival,** BRUGES, BELGIUM Bruges has a reputation for being one of the most beautiful towns in Europe. A silted-up river diminished its important role in commerce starting about 1400, and as a result it's a gorgeous time capsule. And of course the historic glow is improved by the stunning glasses of Belgian beer that can be found at historic cafés like Den Dyver, 't Brugs Beertje, and De Gare. A beer festival is really icing on the cake. The local tasters' group Brugse Autonome Bierproevers organizes a really tasty event. First weekend of February.

*This event ties in perfectly with an organized tour centered on lambics in and around Brussels.*

## BeerTrips: A Week-Long Lambic-sploration,

BRUSSELS, BELGIUM Organized tours offer a lot: transportation, special access to places you'd never think of or get into on your own, a lot of inside information, and the camaraderie of traveling with like-minded beer geeks. BeerTrips has been doing beer tours all over the place for years now, so if you like the sound of this one, check out BeerTrip's other offerings in Europe and elsewhere. And of course there are other tour companies offering similar excursions. This particular one rolls the second week of February.

## The CAMRA National Winter Ales Festival,

MANCHESTER, ENGLAND Winter beers are a lovely specialty in England; we don't get enough of their subtle, warming charms here. The setting here is Manchester, in England's industrial north, which has a burgeoning artisan brewing scene. Beyond the fest, soak up the pub culture and look for local beers like J W Lees, Thwaites, Blackedge, Deeply Vale, Marble, Wilson Potter, First Chop, and Quantum. Third weekend.

*If you can't swing Europe this time around, or if you just haven't had enough barleywine yet:*

## Toronado Barleywine Festival, SAN FRANCISCO,

CALIFORNIA Publican and craft beer pioneer David Keens has been running this well-regarded fest in his bar for more than two decades. It's one of the crown jewels of San Francisco Beer Week, but be prepared to be elbow to elbow with fellow enthusiasts, which is rarely a problem after a couple of big beers. Plenty of great things are happening always in SF, and even more so this week, so you'd better have a plan!

## Pianetta Birra, RIMINI, ITALY

It feels a little like a beer festival, but it's actually the all-Italy bar and nightclub show, with lots of booths showcasing Italy's exciting new craft beer scene. It's also the judging site for Birra del' Anno, Italy's annual craft beer competition. Rimini is a beach town on the Adriatic. There are a few nice beer bars in this ancient Roman town, and there is very little bad food in Italy, so enjoy. End of the month.

**ROUNDUP of March EVENTS**

**Starkbierfest,** MUNICH, GERMANY This event is sort of the strong, dark fraternal twin to Oktoberfest. Taking place partly in the participating breweries' cellars, it showcases the rich, strong, and malty bockbiers, the barleywine equivalents in the lager tradition. *Stark* simply means "strong," and the locals are happy to let off a little steam after a long winter, so expect things to get a bit crazy. The fest is spread around Munich in breweries and beer halls, especially Paulaner's Nockherberg Brewery. As with Oktoberfest, reservations for tables are recommended for larger groups. First two weeks of March.

*If you're thinking of heading back to the States, there's a twofer in Boston on adjacent weekends:*

**Extreme Beer Fest** (EBF), BOSTON, MASSACHUSETTS at the Seaport World Trade Center in Boston. Third weekend.
*And:*

**New England Real Ale eXhibition** (NERAX), BOSTON, MASSACHUSETTS North America's premier celebration of real ale, at the end of the month.

*Boston has a ton of fascinating history and plenty of craft beer watering holes, but the Public House is probably first and foremost among them. Do not miss Cambridge Brewing, one of the more inventive breweries on the planet. Don't forget Boston Beer Company and Harpoon.*

**CELEBRATE: Michael Jackson's Birthday, March 27** This celebrated beer writer really helped build the foundation of a strong and lively craft brewing movement worldwide, and he championed it ferociously until his death in 2007. Doubtless there are many places that will celebrate his birthday, but the most personal might be the Andover Arms in Hammersmith, London, the pub he considered to be his local, and the spot where he enjoyed many pints of his beloved Fuller's Chiswick Bitter over the years. Wherever you are, hoist a pint of your favorite to this genial giant.

**CELEBRATE: King Gambrinus's Birthday, April 11** This fictitious King of Beer has a birthday, but it's not been widely celebrated. Time for a new tradition, I think.

*If you're still in Europe, there's one more major festival this season:*

## Zythos Beer Festival,

LEUVEN, BELGIUM Leuven is a college town just southeast of Brussels, with a huge ancient city square lined with fabulous beer bars. How do you improve on that? Add the most famous beer festival in Belgium and enjoy. Last weekend of the month.

*Or plan a layover in Chicago on your way to California for this free-wheeling thrash:*

## Dark Lord Day, NORTHERN

INDIANA Despite its nondescript location in an industrial park in northern Indiana on the far outskirts of Chicago, the party is as colorful as it gets. Hordes of the young, hip, tattooed, and, above all, beer-obsessed descend on the Three Floyds brewery to scoop up their annual allotment of the legendary Dark Lord Imperial Stout and other goodies offered by the brewery only on the last Saturday in April. The right to purchase bottles of the prized nectar is determined by an online lottery well in advance of the event. Dark Lord Day is a carnival of all things beery, with plenty of draft beer, ad hoc tasting circles (bring your rare beer to share and you'll be in), food, head-banging music, and much more.

**ROUNDUP MAY EVENTS**

*This next one you can celebrate almost anywhere you happen to be:*

### National Homebrew Day and AHA Big Brew

This is a celebration of homebrew that takes place at sites all over North America and beyond. The format is basic: Bring your brewing equipment to wherever the party is, set up and brew a beer, and enjoy the unmatched camaraderie of the homebrew brethren and sisters, plus food and whatever else homebrewers do when they get together and aren't actually brewing. The American Homebrewers Association sponsors the event; go to their website (homebrewersassociation.org) for a listing of locations. Be prepared to make a lot of new friends.

*However, if you can get to southern California, there's no better place to spend National Homebrew Day than at this monster campout:*

### Southern California Homebrewers Festival,

**LAKE CASITAS, CALIFORNIA** This huge outdoor spectacle has been running for a couple of decades now and has grown to well over 2,000 attendees. There is brewing, seminars on a myriad of homebrewing topics, and food, but the highlight is a big beer festival with elaborate club booths serving hundreds of fantastic homebrews. At night, there is a lot of drinking around the campfire. Shuttles to hotels in nearby Ojai (north of Los Angeles) are available. The event is open solely to members of the Southern California Homebrewers Association, but anyone can join the club — so do. First weekend.

*Depending on timing, you may be able to squeeze this one into your itinerary:*

### CELEBRATE: Fred Eckhardt's Birthday, May 10

If you don't know Fred, you should, because he's one of the reasons we have such a lively and irreverent craft beer scene these days. Writer, sage, sake enthusiast, and an exquisite gentleman, his birthday is celebrated with a charity event called FredFest, in his Portland, Oregon, hometown.

*Scoot back across the country for this one-of-a-kind beer and food event:*

## SAVOR: An American Craft Beer & Food Experience,

WASHINGTON, D.C. I hope you're hungry. The Brewers Association lays out a lavish spread for one of the most elegant and upscale beer events around. Designed to showcase how the great flavors of beer and food can raise the experience to lofty heights, the event features dozens of breweries and more beers than you can possibly taste, along with bite-size portions of tasty tidbits on every table. An added benefit is that brewers and owners are required to staff their booths, so it's a great opportunity to chat up some of your idols. Event locations (some years it is held in NYC) and dates change to some degree, but usually it's held around the second weekend.

*Get on a jet and prepare yourself for a couple of long hauls, as the next couple of stops are across the vast Pacific. At least you'll have a soul-soothing stop in the Hawaiian Islands to break up the outbound leg.*

## Maui Brewers Festival,

MAUI, HAWAII It's not the biggest beerfest. Or the one with the wildest, strongest, or most unattainable beers. But it's *Maui*, folks, and the beautiful setting and happy island vibe make this one unique in all the world, tasty local beers included. Third weekend.

## Great Australasian Beer SpecTAPular, MELBOURNE,

AUSTRALIA The Australian beer scene has a slightly different, more businesslike flavor than the North American one, but it's a lot of fun, and the beers are getting more imaginative and assertive as time goes on. This is a great opportunity to survey the scene, including beers from Tasmania and New Zealand and the cutting-edge beers of Western Australia. Melbourne is charming, widely viewed as the best food city Down Under, and as easy a town as there is to navigate. Be sure to get down to the sprawling Victoria Market to shop for

everything from unusual varietal honeys to precious opals.

*If you're still in North America, here's another one that you can enjoy pretty much wherever you happen to be:*

**CELEBRATE: American Craft Beer Week** This a week set aside as a celebration of craft beer by the Brewers Association. Check the craftbeer.com website for a complete listing of hundreds of events across the continent, and for the timing of the nationwide toast in honor of our favorite beverage. Around the third week.

*This schedule gives you plenty of time to rest and make your way to Philadelphia for the best beer week of them all:*

### Philly Beer Week, Philadelphia, Pennsylvania
If you're only going to do one beer week, this is the one. As the original, it's bigger and better organized than many, and there are hundreds of events to scratch any imaginable beery itch. Philly's fun and a great town for food and drink anyway; this just adds dramatically. Be sure to get down to South Philly and explore the Italian markets there, especially the fantastic DiBruno Brothers. Great local foods are also available at the Reading Terminal Market downtown. And, of course, Philadelphia is filled with history and some really great museums, and great local breweries as well. Philly Beer Week occupies 10 jam-packed days starting at the end of May and through the first week of June.

*Get yourself on up to Montreal, Quebec, for this merveilleux event:*

### Mondial de la Bière, Montreal, Quebec, Canada
Quebec has a really exciting beer scene that is built on the unique culinary foundation of its Francophone society. It's craft beer for sure, but there is a strong Belgian sensibility, making it one of my favorite places to drink beer on the continent. Since 1993, Mondial president Jeannine Marois has done a great job of making this one of the most enjoyable events on the globe. It's a typical

fest layout, but it's partly inside and partly outside and it seems a lot less crowded and frantic than the typical fest. Be sure to get out and enjoy Montreal's culture, especially the really fantastic public markets and their selection of local cheeses and charcuterie, and of course brewpubs like Cheval Blanc, Dieu du Ciel!, and others. If you have time, jump across the river to Unibroue in Chambly. Usually early June.

## American Homebrewers Association National Homebrewers Conference,

VARIOUS LOCATIONS If you haven't noticed, homebrewing is big these days. And this event has gone from a few dozen guys sitting around a hotel sharing brews to a large, entertaining, and very well-organized event for several thousand rabid homebrewers.

It's a standard conference format, with presentations during the day and events at night including a local Pro Brewers Night. The highlight is Club Night, a self-assembling beerfest featuring elaborate club booths and costumed crews, and of course hundreds of deliciously creative homebrews for sampling. Always about the middle of June; location rotates around the U.S.

*If you're looking for a more exotic locale for your homebrewing fun, head south:*

## Brazilian National Homebrewing Conference,

VARIOUS LOCATIONS, BRAZIL While the movement is still small, Brazil is exploding with beer enthusiasm these days, and this conference reflects that energy. The format includes competition

judging, seminars, keynotes, great food, plenty of homebrew, and a commercial beer festival. Brazil can be daunting as a travel destination, but when you're hanging with the local homebrewers, there's no more comfortable place to be. They are hungry for a taste of the U.S. craft beer scene, so show up with some interesting bottles and you'll make new friends very quickly. The event moves around Brazil, so check the website of AcervA (acerva.com.br), the national homebrewing club that hosts it. The language of the conference is Portuguese but there are plenty of people around who speak English who will help you make sense of things.

*Back across the Atlantic for:*

### Carnivale Brettanomyces & Andere Wilde Dieren Beer Festival, AMSTERDAM, NETHERLANDS This is a wild

weekend of beer, but one focusing on the beer-transforming micro-organisms rather than the revelers. Taking place in bars and breweries in central Amsterdam on a Friday and Saturday in early July, it's a hardcore mix of professional symposium and beer-tasting event featuring, as the name suggests, beers fermented with *Brettanomyces* and other wild critters, resulting in funky and sour flavors that you either love or hate. Bring your Pepcid. Programs are mostly in Dutch, but beer is a universal language. Amsterdam has plenty of charms: canals, historic buildings, great museums, a vibrant and experimental jazz scene, and amazingly friendly people, so be sure to set aside some time to get out and explore. An all-day canal boat pass is a great way to get around the historic areas.

*Bum around Europe for the rest of the month, building an itinerary around beer events like:*

ArtBeerFest in Caminha, Portugal; the Farsons Great Beer Festival in Ta' Qali, Malta; Festival na pivoto Prilep, Republic of Macedonia; Great Japan Beer Festival, Osaka, Japan; Fête de la Bière, Felletin, France; Pivo in Cvetje, Laško, Slovenia;

Õllesummer festival, Tallinn, Estonia; Tbilisi Beer Fest, Tbilisi, Republic of Georgia.

*Amidst your travels, this one looks like a gem:*

## Scottish Real Ale Festival,

EDINBURGH, SCOTLAND A Scottish take on Britain's classic beer in the beautiful, friendly, and history-drenched Edinburgh, midmonth. If you're a whisky enthusiast, don't miss this opportunity to visit the Scotch Malt Whisky Society tasting room in Leith, the old shipping warehouse district.

*Eventually, you can bookend the month with another great Belgian fest:*

## Beer Passion Weekend,

ANTWERP, BELGIUM A fest organized by *Beer Passion* magazine,

Belgium's best beer journal. End of the month.

*Or, if you just can't seem to get enough homebrewing, swing through Chicago:*

## Siebel Advanced Homebrewing Program,

CHICAGO, ILLINOIS This is a week-long immersive boot camp in late July for homebrewers at the Siebel Institute, taught by a well-known crew of experts and authors. Chicago's a world-class city with an exploding beer scene and a long-established foodie culture. Great art, music, museums, people, everything really — except the traffic.

*If you're not into the homebrewing scene, then this will be more to your taste:*

## Oregon Brewers Festival,

PORTLAND, OREGON This is one of the premier beer festivals in North America. Hosted by the Oregon Craft Brewers Guild since 1988, it takes place in a grassy downtown park under tents and features the best of Pacific Northwest brews. Start at the huge Saturday market nearby for some sustenance and a little shopping, then hit the fest. Portland's a compact and easy-to-navigate town, and just chock-full of brewpubs and beer bars, so don't just breeze in and out for the festival. Stay at one of the McMenamin brewpub hotels in the area, and maybe enjoy a little sightseeing and beer drinking up the gorgeous Columbia River Valley. The event runs the last weekend of the month.

*You can either continue the trail of smaller beer events in Europe like:*

Fête de la Bière, in Schiltigheim, in France's highly gastronomic Alsace region; Belgrade Beer Fest, Belgrade, Serbia; or Dani Piva in Karlovac, Croatia.

*Then wind up at the definitive celebration of real ale on the planet:*

### Great British Beer Festival, LONDON, ENGLAND

The real ale preservationist group CAMRA (Campaign for Real Ale) has been putting on this huge event since 1977 as a way to present the fantastic beers that form an important part of Britain's cultural heritage. Unlike other fests, beer at GBBF is sold by the pint or the half-pint, so be prepared to share with your friends. Takes place over five days midmonth.

*Or if you've had your fill of Europe by now, head back to a super-chill event in Wisconsin:*

### Great Taste of the Midwest, MADISON, WISCONSIN

This is generally regarded as the best summer beer event in the Midwest. The organizers, Madison Homebrewers and Tasters Guild, do a great job of keeping an uncrowded, noncommercial vibe going. The shaded, grassy location next to Madison's Lake Monona doesn't hurt either. Watch out for the many special tappings of rare beers throughout the day, and get in line. Madison is a charming college town with a strong pub culture and several great breweries and brewpubs to visit as well as one of the best farmers' markets in the Midwest, famous for its artisan cheese. If you have time, be sure to stop by New Glarus Brewing Company, a half hour away in a small town with a strong Swiss heritage. Second Saturday.

## ROUNDUP September EVENTS

*Still in Europe? There's one more premier event to add to your collection:*

### Belgian Beer Weekend,

BRUSSELS, BELGIUM Bathe yourself in the glory of a beerfest with more than 400 Belgian beers, held in the Grand Place/Grote Markt. What more can I say? Held on an early weekend in September.

*And then you could probably zip on over to this nearby one in southwest Belgium:*

### Hops Festival/Beer & Food Event, BRASSERIE BROOTCOORENS, ERQUELINNES, BELGIUM Early September.

*And, of course, there's plenty to explore on the route from there*

*through England and a short hop across the water to Ireland:*

## All-Ireland Craft Beer Festival, DUBLIN, IRELAND

Ireland's craft beer scene is rapidly picking up steam, and this fest offers one-stop shopping to try it all out. Midmonth.

*But on the other hand, you just may want to scamper back to North America for this string of pearls on the West Coast:*

## The Great Canadian Beerfest, VICTORIA, BRITISH COLUMBIA, CANADA

British Columbia, in western Canada, has been on the craft beer track for a while now, and it has an especially rich vein of classic cask ales. Located a short ferry hop from Washington's Olympic Peninsula, this beerfest is a great opportunity to get yourself a taste of what's going on in the region. End of the first week of September.

*Then slide down the coast, make a left turn in Seattle, and head over to eastern Oregon for a deep immersion in the aromatic world of hops:*

## Hop & Brew School, YAKIMA, WASHINGTON

Yakima is the epicenter of hop growing in North America. Join the experts at the hop merchant HopUnion for a seminar and celebration of our favorite plant, and see the fascinating agriculture and processing of this green gold. Mid-September.

*A stunningly beautiful 650-mile drive through one of the most brewery-rich corridors in the world eventually lands you here:*

## Northern California Homebrewers Festival, DOBBINS, CALIFORNIA

This event is similar in concept to the homebrewers event in southern California, but with the uniquely laid-back atmosphere offered by northern California. Plenty of great homebrew and a strong focus on food as well. At a camping resort/lake, but hotel lodging is also available. Around the third weekend of the month.

*Or do the grand tour all the way down the incomparable Big Sur coast and end up here after stopping at about a hundred breweries:*

## LA Beer Week, LOS ANGELES, CALIFORNIA

It's not just a Chardonnay town anymore; the beer scene is starting to get very interesting here. Third week of the month.

*Or not, because it's Oktoberfest time:*

## Oktoberfest, MUNICH, GERMANY

You know what I'm talking about. There's no point elaborating about it here, because there's a whole section on it in chapter 5. But you should go. Starts the last week of September and runs for 16 days, well into October.

*Time to get back on that plane again. There are lots of great things happening in North America this time of year. The one wild card is the GABF, which varies as much as a month from year to year, which obviously will change the order of some of your travels.*

Assuming there's no conflict, start in beautiful Seattle for this small but very unusual specialty fest:

## Elysian Brewing's Great Pumpkin Beer Festival, SEATTLE, WASHINGTON

If you're a pumpkin beer freak, there's only one place to be this weekend, and this is it. Early October. See details on page 134.

*If you time things right, you may be able to squeeze in one or more of the harvest-oriented beer festivals that happen this month as you slide on down the West Coast:*

## Wet-Hop Beer Festivals:

Hood River Hops Fest, Hood River, Oregon; Fresh-Hop Ale Festival, Yakima, Washington; San Diego Brewer's Guild Wet Hop Beer Festival, San Diego, California; Portland Fresh Hops Beer Festival, Portland, Oregon.

*But eventually, all roads lead to Denver:*

## Great American Beer Festival, DENVER, COLORADO

You're not really a fully experienced beer geek until you hit this monster of a fest. Dates change from year to year depending on convention center availability. See a much more detailed description on page 131. Plenty of special events, brewery open houses, and more in the whole Front Range area during this week.

*Head southeast, and you'll eventually hit this legendary blowout:*

## The Dixie Cup Homebrew Competition Featuring the Fred Eckhardt Tasting, HOUSTON, TEXAS

A total blast of a homebrew lost weekend. Much more than your usual homebrew competition, even if it is the largest single-site one in the world. Enjoy potluck, homebrew, special Fred Eckhardt beer and food tasting, and a come-in-your-bathrobe barleywine tasting on Saturday morning. Friday and Saturday, midmonth. Try to squeeze in a trip to St. Arnold Brewing Company for a tour and a beer.

*Or if you prefer to have others make your beer for you, it would be best to head back to the Midwest:*

## Cleveland Beer Week, CLEVELAND, OHIO

This one is starting to build some real momentum, connecting nicely with Cleveland's burgeoning food scene. Runs for 10 days starting midmonth.

## Surly Brewing Co. Darkness Day, BROOKLYN CENTER, MINNESOTA

A beer tasting and release for this nearly unobtainable imperial stout. Takes place at Surly Brewing Co. on a Saturday near the end of the month.

*You're probably getting whiplash from the transatlantic crossings by now, but I promise you that this one is really worth it:*

## Salone del Gusto, TORINO, ITALY

An enormous food festival so fabulous that you'll forget all about beer. But just in case you don't, there's plenty of that to choose from amongst the cheese, wine and *salumi*, especially from Italy's highly creative craft beer scene. Torino is a beautiful Victorian city with polite people, a large confectionery industry, a great museum of Egyptian antiquities, and oh yes, the church with that shroud thing in its basement. As the capital of Piemonte, one of Italy's premier wine regions, Torino's food and drink are extra awesome. Be sure to try the frizzante Barbera red wine with dinner. Gorgeous scenery, too, and at this time of year it's harvest season. If this isn't heaven, I'm hard-pressed to figure out what is. Late in the month. Find more information on page 127.

*If you can drag yourself back to the West Coast — or if you never left — it's time for a little fun in the sun:*

## San Diego Beer Week,

SAN DIEGO, CALIFORNIA A great outpouring of beery fun from a town already gushing with great beer — as long as you are okay with hops.

While you're there, catch the San Diego Brewers Guild Beer Festival. Besides appreciating the beaches, seafood, and awesome weather, be sure to get out and enjoy some of the world-class breweries in the area: Green Flash, Pizza Port, Ballast Point AleSmith, and the astonishingly grand brewpub (or should I say brewtemple) Stone Brewing Co., along with a ton of new small ones. The beer week is held early in the month.

*Hop on Amtrak's California Zephyr for a leisurely ride through the beautiful scenery of America's Southwest and you'll wind up in Chicago, refreshed and ready for:*

## Festival of Barrel-Aged Beer, CHICAGO, ILLINOIS

Focusing exclusively on beers that have had an intimate encounter with something woody, FOBAB is a connoisseur's delight of the rare and

exotic, featuring everything from the massive bourbon-aged stouts that got this category going to delicate wine barrel–aged farmhouse ales and everything in between. Presented by the Illinois Craft Brewers Guild around the second Saturday in November.

*While you're in Chicago, the timing will probably work out for you to immerse yourself the week before in some professional training at the world-famous Siebel Institute brewing school:*

### Siebel Master of Beer Styles and Evaluation,

CHICAGO, ILLINOIS This is several days of intense tasting, smelling, and learning about the flavors of beer, the history and characteristics of most of the classic styles, and how to best formulate and brew them. Siebel Institute, near downtown.

*You may be getting just a teensy bit tired by this point, but if you're not*

*yet hospitalized from fatigue — or worse — you might want to grab an IV bag or two and add a couple more events to your journey:*

### Portland Holiday Beer Festival, PORTLAND, OREGON

It is what it sounds like: a grand celebration of holiday beers of all stripes, held in the comfort of heated tents in downtown Portland. Check out plenty of special editions and one-offs from local breweries, unlikely to be found anywhere else on earth. Early December.

### Kerstbier Fest, ESSEN,

BELGIUM One final event for you, the Christmas Beer Festival, this time with deliriously tasty and strong Belgian Christmas beers. Six nights, five days, midmonth in Essen, near Antwerp.

*Whew.*

*Just a couple of weeks to rest a little and prepare to shower your friends and family with the fabulous beers and other gifts you've collected on your world travels.*

*I hope you enjoyed your trip. I wish I could have been there drinking beer with you.*

# INDEX

# Y

# Z

# PHOTOGRAPHY CREDITS

# OTHER STOREY BEER TITLES YOU WILL ENJOY

## ALSO BY RANDY MOSHER

### Tasting Beer

Everyone knows how to drink beer, but do you know how to taste it? Now you can uncap the secrets in every bottle of the world's greatest drink and gain an understanding of the finer points of brewing, serving, tasting, and food pairing. You'll discover the ingredients and brewing methods that make each brew unique and learn to identify the scents, colors, flavors, and mouthfeel of all the major beer styles. Mosher offers recommendations for brews to try in more than 50 beer styles from around the world.
256 pages. Paper.
ISBN 978-1-60342-089-1.

### The American Craft Beer Cookbook
by John Holl

The pleasure of going to a craft brewery for a pint and a delicious meal can now be re-created at home with this collection of 155 recipes. From pub grub and barbecue to regional specialties and even breakfast fare, many of these dishes use beer as an ingredient, and all taste amazingly great with beer. The recipes were contributed by brewpubs and craft brewers across the United States.
352 pages. Paper. ISBN 978-1-61212-090-4.

### The Secret Life of Beer! by Alan D. Eames

The secrets and mysteries of beer are revealed in this intriguing book of cultural history, poetry, song, little-known facts, and quirky quotes by beer drinkers from Nietzsche to Darwin.
384 pages. Paper. ISBN 978-1-58017-601-9.

### Vintage Beer by Patrick Dawson

Certain beers can be aged, a process that enhances and changes their flavors in interesting and delicious ways. Patrick Dawson explains how to identify a cellar-worthy beer, how to set up a beer cellar, what to look for when tasting vintage beers, and the fascinating science behind the aging process.
160 pages. Paper. ISBN 978-1-61212-156-7.

---

*These and other books from Storey Publishing are available wherever quality books are sold or by calling 1-800-441-5700.*
*Visit us at www.storey.com or sign up for our newsletter at www.storey.com/signup.*